Ruling or Serving Society?

Shahid Ahmed

Ruling or Serving Society?

The Case for Reforming Financial Services

palgrave
macmillan

Shahid Ahmed
UN Economic and Social Commission
for Asia and the Pacific
Bangkok, Thailand

ISBN 978-3-030-00520-7 ISBN 978-3-030-00521-4 (eBook)
https://doi.org/10.1007/978-3-030-00521-4

Library of Congress Control Number: 2018957070

This Palgrave Macmillan imprint is published by the registered company Springer Nature Switzerland AG
The registered company address is: Gewerbestrasse 11, 6330 Cham, Switzerland

Preface

The 2007/08 financial crisis, following other less-severe financial crises in the 1980s and 1990s, revealed that all economies, developed and developing, had become dangerously vulnerable to the way financial services had operated during the last three decades.[1] Not so long ago, conventional Economics textbooks taught students that the primary purpose of economic activity was the production of goods and services in response to the demand emanating from society. Producers of goods and services combined the factors of production, i.e. land, labour and capital, in the most efficient way possible and then provided their output to society, in competition with others. The principal, if not exclusive, function of finance was to intermediate between savers, on the one hand, and investors, on the other, to provide the funds required by the producers but always keeping in view its fiduciary duties. More recently, i.e. since the 1970s, intermediation has also extended to financing longer-term household mortgages and personal consumption.

Over the last three decades, however, as neoliberal ideas and globalization have gained intellectual ascendancy, there has been unrelenting pressure to redefine the role of the State in support of corporate profit making by deregulating, marketizing and privatizing an increasing array of economic activities. In the process, economies have become

[1] Financial services are defined here as retail and wholesale, i.e. investment, banks, capital markets, insurance companies, fund management and hedge funds.

financialized[2] and finance now plays a far bigger role in all economies than in the 1960s, irrespective of the level of development,[3] and has acquired a size and complexity that goes well beyond mere intermediation. What have been the consequences of this development?

At the most visible level, there has been an explosion of indebtedness. Recent estimates for global GDP are of the order of $75 trillion while the figure for global debt stock is over three times that. At the same time, cross-border investment flows, FDI and bank lending, have risen from about two-thirds of global GDP in 1980 to more than four times in 2015—even for developing countries such flows have doubled during this period. Generally speaking, financial services in the aggregate have grown much faster than the rest of the economy over the last 30 years on a global basis.[4] But, these phenomena have brought few, if any, worthwhile benefits. More people can, and do, access finance but against that, overall output growth has not accelerated, indebtedness has increased, and income distribution and inequality have worsened. The more integrated global economy has witnessed a large increase in imbalances and in chronic instability in the shape of asset bubbles, especially with the involvement of very large institutions in the speculative trading of massive volumes of increasingly esoteric securities.

Neither in the developed nor in the developing countries have many questioned the need for this huge increase in financial-sector activity and its attendant side-effects. Indeed, it has been given a relatively neutral name 'financial deepening' and accepted not just as part of the natural order of things but assumed to be beneficial. It is not coincidental, however, that the increase has also generated the means that have facilitated rent-seeking behaviour in finance with a significant portion of these rents finding their way into the media, universities and think tanks, thus indirectly promoting and giving sustenance to a pro-neoliberal climate of opinion. For instance, neoliberal maxims continue to be routinely taught in Economics and Business courses across the world as self-evident truths and the media, for their part, paint a picture that the all-pervasive

[2] The term financialization has been defined in different ways by different people. Broadly speaking, it refers to the increasing importance of financial services in the economy.

[3] By and large, financial services have doubled in size relative to other sectors of the economy in most developed countries and in most middle-income developing countries. However, their contribution to gross corporate profits is much bigger.

[4] Figures derived from a mixture of OECD, IMF and BIS data.

importance of finance is in fact a boon for the economy. Given that bank credit is based to a significant degree on created money, the underlying risks of misjudgements and of moral hazard to the wider economy in this are very real, as the world has discovered post-2008, but are little discussed or, for that matter, adequately appreciated.

Against this background, there is a prima facie need to better understand how such a State of affairs has been reached, what are its wider implications for equitable economic and social development, where would the forces driving it might take us if allowed to continue unchecked and what action is needed to mitigate its worst effects. For now, at any rate, there is little or no consensus regarding the answers to these questions. Although the warnings by Keynes (and others) in the 1920s and 1930s about the dangers of downgrading the public interest to the margins in any economy and leaving it to the unfettered operations of markets to deliver desirable economic and social outcomes have acquired a new relevance, they have not really become mainstream. The Governor of the Bank of England was quoted as saying in the Guardian (July 4, 2017) that 'a decade after the start of the global financial crisis G20 reforms are building a safer, simpler and fairer financial system…and that we have fixed the issues that caused the last crisis'. Not many, however, would share the Governor's optimism. Indeed, most feel that as indebtedness continues to increase another financial crisis is only a matter of time.[5]

Led by the global institutional set-up (World Bank, IMF, OECD, regional development banks, the Financial Stability Board and an array of satellite think tanks), developing economies have also accepted the nostrums of marketization and financialization. Nevertheless, some countries, notably China and to some extent India, still have financial systems that are largely publicly owned and the priorities of public policy in these and some other countries have not elevated finance to pre-eminence as they have, say, in the UK and USA. But in a globalized world even these economies have shown signs of financialization and anyway cannot shield themselves entirely from the risks and instability emerging in the developed countries. The need for both national and international action to make finance safer and much more responsive to the needs of

[5] Ten years after the crisis, overall levels of indebtedness in the USA, EU (eurozone) and the UK remain the same or have increased. The indebtedness has shifted from the banking system to governments, households and corporations.

society is thus inescapable. Nationally, developing economies need to firmly stamp the overriding importance of the public interest on financial services. Internationally, side by side with ongoing initiatives at the BIS (Basel III for instance), developing economies need to work towards a more democratized, less-laissez-faire, international financial system with robust programmes of socially responsible regulation and reform. In this regard, the case of the Bank of Credit and Commerce International (1972–1991) provides useful insights into how otherwise well-meaning attempts originating in the developing countries to widen the provision of financial services can end in failure when both the individual institution and its regulators lack a clear-cut, socially attuned operational framework (see Chapter 3). Internationally, side by side with ongoing initiatives at the BIS, developing countries need to work towards a more democratized, less-laissez-faire, more robust, system of socially progressive regulation and reform, the main elements of which are discussed in the concluding chapter.

It is worth recalling that many years ago, the UK established two high-powered Committees, the Macmillan Committee on Finance and Industry in 1931 (in which Keynes played a major part) in the wake of the 1929 crash and in 1959, the Radcliffe Committee on the Working of the Monetary System to improve post-War economic performance (see Chapter 2). The financial sector benefited from the diversity of views that these committees brought to bear on its functions and overall objectives but more fundamentally both committees established that finance was there to service the real economy and society and not the other way round. Now, something similar is needed so that countries might know what a liberalized, and still unreformed, financial sector entails in terms of risks, costs and benefits.

The key point facing governments and society today is that there is a large gap in the everyday perception of money and banks and the surrounding reality in terms of their extraordinary hold over the collective resources of a country and this gap needs to be narrowed. While everyone has to deal with finance on a daily basis, very few comprehend its complexities or are aware of its fragile foundations. Finance is not run by geniuses, evil or enlightened, its complexities are man-made and the notion 'too big to fail' facilitates excessive risk-taking and rent-seeking behaviour in the sector. Greed and hubris, alas, can affect even the most gifted in the sector and make decision-making casual and irresponsible. Regrettably, what most people read in newspapers or see and hear on TV or radio leaves them none the wiser and so-called experts often ply their own biases and prejudices as scientific truths. Following the 2007/08 crisis, the reform effort has produced no fundamental change in the institutional arrangements covering finance; indeed, most reform proposals have fallen well short of the radical changes that are actually needed to make it safer (Wolf 2014). In fact, if truth be told, financial services have been given, perhaps inadvertently, yet another lifeline of cheap liquidity, this time from the central banks in the form of QE, to be recycled through a complex array of financial instruments into a debt-addicted economy, populated by an unsuspecting public, in yet more indebtedness.[6] This book on its own would obviously not be able to fill the wide gaps in knowledge or understanding that exist amongst the general public, but it could contribute to a more informed debate on both what should be done now and what the finance sector is ultimately for.

Bangkok, Thailand Shahid Ahmed

[6] There is certainly greater understanding of the causes of the 2007/08 crisis. However, there is little or no appreciation of the dangers of building another fragile recovery on debt and speculation.

Acknowledgements

Over my working life which began in Pakistan's central bank, the *State Bank of Pakistan*, followed by a decade and a half at the *Bank of Credit and Commerce International* and ended with the *United Nations Economic and Social Commission for Asia and the Pacific*, a period I had ample opportunity to observe financial-sector operations at first hand and to try and understand what role, if any, the sector played in development as I witnessed the 1997 financial crisis in Southeast Asia which led to large output losses and a substantial increase in unemployment in several countries. I also had an opportunity to participate in the application of both the theoretical precepts of Economics and lessons drawn from the vast empirical research that the subject had generated across the world. In both instances, the experience was less than edifying. It seemed to me that as professional economists we were, almost always, only tinkering with solutions to problems.

In Economics, we talk of efficient financial markets but the financial sector itself adds a major and unnecessary element of instability into the real economy. Moreover, its role in development is limited at best. For instance, access to financial services is hopelessly skewed and credit to enterprises with high rates of social return is usually denied. Start-ups struggle to get support. The impact on the wider economy of the financial sector is usually of no concern to the sector. In fact, operating on the basis of herd instinct and creating asset bubbles have been common features in the way financial services have impacted on the real economy in the recent past. The sector's forte for many years has been speculation, which is no different to gambling. Then, within development, on the social side there are the myriad disadvantages of being born poor to which there are no practical solutions within the ambit of conventional economic or financial policies. For the poor, the great bulk of financial services are barely relevant, their access being primarily through usurious payday loans. Indeed, on the social front without well-targeted, sustained direct State intervention, nothing can be done to overcome the disadvantages of being born in an underprivileged household in most societies.

Given all this, it seemed to me then that we were essentially doing repair jobs in our professional work to keep the house livable despite knowing that its foundations were weak. By foundations, I mean the reality of unequal political power in society and how it impinges upon the functioning of society and how the powerful are able to weave a supporting narrative that enables them to exercise almost complete control over society's collective resources. Over time, it became obvious to me, for example, that in countries like Pakistan why the fundamental issue of poverty has remained unaddressed was not down to errors in policymaking but more to the unequal distribution of power in society and how this had allowed the needs of the less fortunate to be effectively ignored. This had bred, in turn, a sense of resignation and apathy across wide sections of society in the country leaving the field open to a political process based on cant, humbug and hypocrisy.

During my time at University in Britain in the 1960s, I had been deeply impressed by the ideas of Joan Robinson. In two small books, *Economic Philosophy* and *Freedom and Necessity*, she provided powerful explanations of how societies evolve, how their value systems evolve, sometimes for the worse, how they get to be what they are and how political and, indeed, intellectual victories are never final—witness how siren voices in the UK are beginning to say openly in 2018 that the welfare State is unaffordable. Inspired by her, I acquired a profound desire to place the study of Economics within the larger corpus of social and political issues that all countries face to a greater or lesser extent.

For many years after starting my professional career, I genuinely believed that the problems of poverty, inequality and social justice had been largely solved in countries like Britain. Where action was needed were countries like Pakistan, the land of my birth. But I fear that in Britain, where I live, the post-war social contract is fraying in front of our eyes. It is a sad reality that the State is no longer a protector of the weak but is blithely acquiescent in allowing tax havens to flourish while offering nothing but platitudes as budgets for education, the care of the elderly and health are cut. Meanwhile, the financial sector flourishes with taxpayers' money. With a deep sense of humility, I should like to dedicate this book to Joan Robinson. It is her writings that have given me the tools to explain the world in the way that I have sought to do in this book.

Books are the products of discussions with countless individuals whose ideas have shed light on the world in all its complexity; not all of them can be remembered and thanked individually but honesty demands that I acknowledge the debt that I owe to them. In addition, my friends, Richard Kozul-Wright of UNCTAD in particular, and Bruce Lloyd, Prof. Emeritus at the South Bank University, have patiently read parts of the book in draft form and pointed out areas for improvement as have others who have asked that they not be named. The head of Economics and Finance at Palgrave Macmillan, Rachel Sangster made my job easier than it should have been by responding so positively to my book proposal, thereby giving me the confidence, despite doubts, to sit down and start writing. The comments of an anonymous referee chosen by Palgrave Macmillan were particularly valuable in giving final shape to the book. To all of them, I should like to express my sincere and grateful thanks. But, most of all, I must give my heartfelt thanks to my wife Asifa and to our children, Ali, Maria and Hashim and Ali's wife Michela for their mixture of encouragement, gentle criticism and much practical help in conceiving and writing this book. For an increasingly crotchety old man perhaps not fully aware of his shortcomings, all of them have been towers of strength with their combination of realism and good humour. They have enabled me to finish the book within the deadline given by the publisher. Needless to add, all errors and omissions in the book are my responsibility.

Contents

1 Introduction	1
2 Money, the Real Economy and Financial Services	15
3 Financial Services, Growth and Development	43
4 Financial Services and the Crisis of Capitalism	67
5 The Future: Making Financial Services Subservient to the Needs of Society	83
Bibliography	105
Index	109

CHAPTER 1

Introduction

Abstract The Introduction provides a brief history of the economic role of financial services. It also deals with the traditional intermediation function performed by banks and discusses the evolution of different types of financial institution, including the modern investment bank. It explains the growing importance of securities' trading by banks in the developed countries since 1980 leading to a neglect of their traditional functions and how neoliberal ideas have contributed to the phenomenon of financialization in the developed economies and to the rapid growth of financial services in the world as a whole. However, the Introduction avers that financialization has not only led to a massive increase in the global stock of debt but also to a marked increase in the vulnerability of economies to financial crises.

Keywords Bank failures (G21) · Financial crises (G01)
Financial markets (D53)

Historical Evolution of Financial Services

As soon as economic activity moved beyond barter, rudimentary financial services came into being. Banks had been established in medieval Italy as far back as the fourteenth and fifteenth centuries in response to the trade that started between Italy's different city States and financing such trade and underwriting the risks that accompanied it were the beginnings of

S. Ahmed, *Ruling or Serving Society?*,
https://doi.org/10.1007/978-3-030-00521-4_1

banking as we know it today. Britain followed with similar banks in the seventeenth century. Merchants and artisans and, indeed, anyone with an excess of goods beyond their immediate needs, whether for their own consumption or for sale to others, would convert some or all of them into gold or silver, the only acceptable medium of exchange known at the time. The gold or silver would, in turn, be deposited with gold or silversmiths for safe keeping with the latter issuing receipts in lieu to the depositors. These receipts then began to be used for making payments or for settling debts rather than physically transferring any of the gold or silver for the purpose. The goldsmiths, for their part, would note the changes in ownership of the precious metals on their books. The receipts—essentially pieces of paper backed by the deposited precious metals—were the forerunners of modern paper money. Over time, owners of the receipts began to lend them to friends and associates and such receipts could remain in circulation almost indefinitely being used by their holders (individuals and partnerships) for buying and selling goods and for settling debts, rarely coming back to be exchanged for the deposited gold or silver. In fact, the total of claims outstanding against the original gold or silver at any given time could be several times more than the quantities of the metals actually deposited. Thus, the banking principle was born.

Nowadays, the issuance of paper money is a monopoly of the State while lending money—giving credit[1]—and the price at which it is done, the rate of interest, has become an elaborate activity not only in the variety and number of institutions involved but is governed by its own dedicated framework of practices, conventions, laws and regulations including the establishment of central banks. Economics itself has come up with a field of study called 'monetary theory' that seeks to distinguish the different influences that affect the real and monetary parts of the economy and financial economics is an integral part of any Economics or MBA course. As with other fields of study in Economics the subject is not without its share of disagreements and controversies.

Taking a broad view of the economy all money, i.e. any instrument that allows its holder to exchange it for goods and services, is essentially a matter of credit.[2] Therefore, when an institution overextends its

[1] The word credit is derived from the Latin *creditum* meaning belief or faith.

[2] Money goes beyond the notes and coins issued by the State or central bank otherwise known as legal tender.

credit, and not only to individual customers but also to sister institutions engaged in similar activities, some of the borrowers will inevitably be unable to repay. When this happens the lending institution has effectively lost a part of the money that was deposited with it. Under certain circumstances, this may cause the institution to fail and, given the interconnectedness of lending institutions and individual borrowers in the modern economy, the whole of the lending and borrowing system could be in danger of collapsing. In any modern economy, lending institutions are consequently obliged to keep a portion of the equivalent of the gold or silver (the money deposited with them), as a reserve with another institution. This institution has been called the central bank and given its vital role in maintaining the confidence of the general public its importance was quickly established. Many central banks in the developed countries have been in existence for the better part of three centuries.[3] Today, it would be difficult to imagine a banking system without a central bank. Although central banks initially came into being primarily to provide confidence to depositors, they are now an integral component of the financial system and are directly responsible for maintaining adequate liquidity and price stability in the economy and, in many countries, for regulating the banking system.

It needs to be stressed that money cannot in most economies be precisely measured. The easiest definition is the quantity of money issued as 'legal tender' by the State or central bank. However, money is an elastic entity. It is whatever society is prepared to accept and in history there have been instances of substitutes for money (cigarettes in POW camps in World War II, cowrie shells in the Pacific etc.) From a modern perspective, the simplest form of created money is any IOU that can be discounted in the market. As a result, the financial system can keep on expanding almost indefinitely, so long as confidence is maintained. Indeed, the financial system as a whole can exceed the total value of the output of goods and services in an economy many times over, as it has in a number of countries (Pettifor 2017).

In conventional textbook analysis, the function of a financial system consisting of banking and the issuance and trading of financial assets is essentially to intermediate between those with surplus funds at their disposal which they have deposited with a commercial bank (or other

[3]With the exception of the USA. Here, the Federal Reserve System was created as recently as in 1913.

institutions such as savings banks, building and mutual societies), i.e. savers, and those who might need them for varying periods of time, i.e. borrowers. The quantity of funds that a bank can lend is, however, constrained by two influences: *one*, on the demand side, the number of sound and reliable borrowers and the quality of the security that they can provide against the possibility of default. This is the bank's principal fiduciary responsibility: to assess risk objectively and to lend funds in the least risky way possible so that its legal and moral responsibilities, meaning the safety of the savings in its care, are not compromised. *Two*, on the supply side, it is constrained by its share of the total of society's savings in circulation. A bank may theoretically only lend the savings that have been deposited with it but nothing stops it from borrowing from other banks, at home and abroad, to increase the size of its operations except its own creditworthiness.[4]

As part of the long-term evolution of the financial system it is also worth remembering that as economies began to grow and individuals and enterprises grew richer the need for longer-term funds such as equity or pre-production capital, particularly on the part of enterprises, grew in tandem. In addition to, short-term loans two types of financial instrument came into being: shares and bonds. Shares are a form of part ownership of the enterprise issuing them.[5] The owners of the shares are entitled to receive a part of the profits of that enterprise and to participate in its management by electing its board of directors. Generally speaking, shares have to be held in perpetuity (i.e. till such time as the share-issuing enterprise continues to exist) but holders can sell them on and there is, in fact, an active market in the buying and selling of shares in most countries through the stock exchange. Bonds, on the other hand, are a form of debt and carry an obligation to pay a certain sum of money per annum to their holders. By and large, bonds have an end date, i.e. maturity, when they have to be 'redeemed' or repaid but they, too, are traded like shares before reaching maturity.

As a result of the principle of limited liability both shares and bonds have become vehicles for absorbing the surplus funds of individual

[4]Following globalization it is theoretically possible for any economy to live beyond the limits of its savings by utilizing the surplus savings of other countries. The only caveat is how the savings are then used.

[5]Without going into the technicalities of voting and non-voting shares, legally whoever owns the majority of shares in an enterprise is the owner of that enterprise.

investors, whether households, firms or financial institutions and are as such a form of wealth. But the managers of the enterprises that have issued them are not in existence for satisfying the interests of the share- or bond-holders. They are there to generate a surplus over the costs of all inputs used by them in production, i.e. *make profits for the enterprise*, with which their own interests are aligned. The need to pay out dividends on the shares or interest on the bonds is almost identical but the enterprises will do so to the minimum extent needed, i.e. just enough for the investors to keep them interested. In practical terms, shares and bonds can be considered to be identical as far as the financial needs of an enterprise are concerned and for investors they are merely different ways of earning 'rent'. They do have a separate legal status, and often they are treated differently for tax purposes,[6] but ultimately they are similar ways of raising longer-term finance by enterprises.

The total of finance available in the economy at any given time is the equivalent of all public and private wealth, also embodying physical assets like infrastructure, houses, buildings, plant and machinery. Into this pool flow day by day new surplus funds from savings and profits that are then invested in shares and bonds or are deposited in banks. These incremental flows are, however, small compared to the total stock of financial assets in the economy. Thus, it is very unlikely that the average price of shares and bonds that constitute the aggregate of the pool would be materially affected by the size of these flows. Historically, the main influence on these prices has been the state of expectations which affects not just the price of shares but, indirectly, the rate of interest as well. The latter because the price of has to be low enough, and the yield high enough, in order for them to compete with shares. New bonds can be sold only if they can promise a risk-adjusted return that is comparable to that of shares. Empirically, it has been seen that when banks make more loans they tend to reduce the demand for bonds, so pushing up interest rates.

Financialization

The financial system has evolved into playing a variety of other roles and in the past each of the roles was kept distinct with its own regulatory regime particularly after World War II. For savers, in addition to banks

[6]The favourable tax treatment of debt has been instrumental in a huge increase in corporate indebtedness.

there are insurance companies, building societies, blind trusts, managed funds, hedge funds and pensions, all playing different roles in the economy whether to buy protection against risk or to protect the value of the assets/savings over the long term. For large or wealthy investors there were wholesale banks that primarily operated in the interbank market, dealt with enterprises and/or with large private clients, managed cross-border financial flows and assisted in new and growing avenues for providing finance, such as cross-border trade and investment that gave rise to a separate class of risks, such as exchange rates and political developments. Since the 1980s, the pressure to liberalize and deregulate financial services has blurred the lines of demarcation between these various activities and their role in the economy has expanded many times over, driven in part by the recent ultra-low interest rate environment and the need to boost profits as the profitability of conventional banking has diminished. This has made risk management far more complex. For example, subject to the sensible identification and management of such risks all these activities should be safe and profitable. But what has happened is that banks in their search for growth and profits have proceeded to expand massively into entirely new areas of operations. In the world's principal financial centres, New York, London, Hong Kong, Singapore and Tokyo, issuing and trading in securities has greatly reduced, if not obliterated, their traditional operations. These activities have altered the nature of financial services fundamentally by pushing into the background the fiduciary responsibilities of financial institutions and by greatly incentivising risk-taking behaviour. Roughly from the 1980s onwards, the balance sheets of financial companies have expanded to levels that are difficult to comprehend for the layperson[7] and the risks of losses and instability have correspondingly multiplied to such an extent that the whole of society has become hostage to their activities. This is the main manifestation of the phenomenon of financialization.

It should be remembered that issuing and trading securities is not new. It was already happening in the USA on a significant scale around the Great Depression that began in 1929 and one of the reform measures adopted at the time was the legal separation of retail banking from

[7] The largest banks in the world and the largest investment funds run into hundreds of billions, some into trillions, of dollars.

its riskier cousin, investment banking.[8] In the UK, commercial banking and merchant banking were two distinct areas of activity in the financial sector, albeit with some overlap. What has happened over the past three decades is that 'universal' banking combining the two has emerged virtually across the world. On the investment banking side, the issuance of securities on behalf of an enterprise has become a secondary activity while the invention of and trading in new instruments and 'products' in the financial markets has mushroomed.[9] Most new products are based on complicated mathematical formulae and are theoretically meant to minimize, if not eliminate altogether, all risks involved in holding or trading them. As part of the process of financialization M and A (Mergers and Acquisitions) activity has also expanded. However, as research has shown (Foroohar 2016), such activity is not conducted for any long-term efficiency gains for the companies involved or for the economy but for tax reasons or for stripping assets, share buybacks or for gaining market dominance. In other words, the rationale is financial engineering in which the primary purpose is to generate activity in the sector for its own sake and which enriches the participants in the process.

In the past, a bank made a loan and the loan remained on its books until it was repaid. Now, banks bundle their loans into securities, claim that they are backed by assets and sell them on in the market. Often the yield on these securities is higher than on conventional shares and bonds and, hence, they are attractive investment outlets. Their selling point is that the statistical likelihood of a bundle of, say, thousands of a mix of safe and not-so-safe loans going bad is low and can be fairly realistically estimated; hence, they can be accurately priced and marketed. In this way, relatively dubious assets can be bundled with better quality ones and successfully marketed to provide additional sources of revenue to the issuer. As a result, marginal customers have been able to access the financial system—in marked contrast to the days before liberalization. Credit rating agencies have assisted the marketization of these assets by rating them, and they are paid for their services by the issuing institution, a process that can hardly be described as independent or 'arm's length'. This is not all. Banks have gone further and created instruments called

[8]This is when the Glass-Steagal Act of 1933 was passed by the US Congress separating commercial from investment banking. The Act was repealed in 1999.

[9]It is rather strange that operators in financial services refer to paper assets as 'products' as if they possessed physical characteristics.

'derivatives'. Derivatives possess no intrinsic value of their own. They are primarily used to forecast the impact that events in the future might have on the price of the underlying security. Given these developments a layperson might conclude that financial services are now not only risk-free but can cater to any conceivable demand from an enterprise or the general public.[10] But as the 2007/08 banking crisis showed such a view bears little relationship with reality.

It is worth recalling that the origin of many of these instruments was in the agricultural commodity markets where there was a rational need to know how bad weather, or other similar events, might affect their prices in the future. Forward and futures markets in a host of commodities therefore came into being and played a useful role in minimizing the impact of unforeseen events on their production and prices and producers could protect themselves against precipitate falls in earnings. But these otherwise rational hedging activities were soon overtaken by speculation and attracted persons and institutions with no inherent stake in the commodities themselves to speculate about their prices in the future, often on a staggering scale in terms of the sums of money involved. Traders, regulators and even governments lauded these developments as assisting in the creation of 'deep' and 'liquid' markets. But, in reality they were anything but, causing prices in many markets to fluctuate unnecessarily and magnifying the fluctuations as speculators piled into particular markets on the basis of herd instinct (Silver 2017). In other words, trading in these instruments is effectively nothing but a form of gambling.[11]

A further consequence of the huge growth in investment banking activity has been not only to make the financial system very large vis-à-vis the rest of the economy but much more unstable. In the past, activity in the financial sector would fluctuate in tandem with what was happening in the real economy and understanding the trade or business cycle was the central preoccupation of macroeconomics before and after the arrival of Keynesian economics in the 1930s. Now, it is the financial sector itself that has introduced new and much higher levels of instability in

[10] Merton and Scholes winners of the Nobel Prize in Economics in 1998 had made such a claim.

[11] A form of gambling that when extended to the commodities markets in 2010 caused large increases in food prices and led to considerable distress in the developing countries of South Asia where expenditure on food constitutes a major portion of the spending of the poor.

the economy. In addition to the instability, which is self-evident, the vast growth in securities' trading has impacted on non-financial enterprises as well, as financialization has gathered pace. The most obvious effect of financialization has been to give pre-eminence to short-term profits and to shorten the time horizon within which their managements take decisions. Many, if not most, such enterprises openly participate in financial markets and it appears that preoccupation with short-term profits has led to the neglect of their core activities. The focus on short-term profits, as shareholders have become increasingly impatient, has meant that the average period of shareholding has declined from five years in the 1960s to only a few months now (Kay 2015).[12] This concentration on short-term shareholder value has been far from benign: not only R&D (Research and Development) expenditures but overall investment levels have either flat-lined or have declined over the last two decades (Lazonick 2010). More tellingly, the biggest price has been paid by the workers who have seen their wages stagnate during the last three decades.

The extraordinary growth of financial sector activity since the 1980s has also led to a critical misallocation of scarce human and IT resources in many economies. Some of the brightest young men and women have been drawn into the sector where they have been handsomely rewarded. But, it is a harsh judgment that they have largely wasted their time from a societal perspective.[13] It hardly needs stating that across the world there is a growing shortage of doctors, engineers and scientists and many countries have filled such skill gaps by poaching talent from the developing countries where opportunities and earnings remain constrained. This has created a double problem: the exporting countries have been deprived of the skills on which their societies had invested their limited resources; the importing countries have landed themselves with the intractable social and political problem of 'immigration' and gratuitously raised social tensions, as in the USA and Western Europe.[14]

[12]The Kay Review of UK Equity Markets 2012, www.parliament.uk Publications and records.

[13]All high earners in finance need to ask themselves if their massive compensation packages—often more than the equivalent of 15 times an average teacher's salary—can be justified on rational grounds.

[14]There is near unanimity amongst commentators and social scientists that the Brexit phenomenon in the UK and the election of Donald Trump in the USA have been driven by the scapegoating of immigrants in both countries.

Financial Services in Developing Countries

What of the developing countries?[15] It should be noted here that most developing countries still display a heavy preference for cash. Until the early 1970s, finance played a limited role in development, banks were mostly privately owned and their operations were restricted to short-term support for domestic and foreign trade. Development required long-term funds and few developing countries had access to long-term development funds especially for physical infrastructure. Even payment systems were not widely needed. For many years most developing countries as ex-colonies had relied on foreign-owned banks for the bulk of their banking requirements. With the passage of time, some of these countries set up government-owned banks, including specialist banks for agriculture and industry and later for microfinance in order to broaden the delivery of financial services in the economy. Thereafter, stock markets and the institutions required for regulating the stock markets were also established. In most such countries, the State dominated the sector (as it still does in China and India, less so in other developing countries) and development was based on a rough and ready system of sectoral priorities within an import-substituting strategy.

The underlying idea was that the financial system would successfully convert the savings of society into a financial form and thereby help promote long-term investment in development. In the event, with some notable exceptions in East Asia, it was the State itself that used the financial system for its own needs, sometimes merely to meet the shortfall between the resources it could raise via taxation and its myriad spending commitments. In this way, the financial system provided an easy alternative to the more politically vexatious problem of raising resources by taxing the rich. But, as in the developed countries, irrespective of the level of development prevailing in these economies, the developing economies sought to mimic not just the institutional structure of the more developed countries but also their *modus operandi*. In a short span of time banks in the developing countries had invested in expensive IT systems and were earning an increasing portion of their revenue from speculating in the securities markets often obtaining funds from wholesale sources.

[15] For the purposes of this book developing countries are primarily the larger economies of East, South-East and South Asia, i.e. China, South Korea, Hong Kong, Indonesia, Thailand, Malaysia, Philippines.

This mimicking of the developed countries was given extra impetus as neoliberal ideas gained ground across the world. Following the debt crisis of the early 1980s, many developing countries began to pursue an agenda based on reducing the role of the State, privatizing publicly owned assets, lowering taxes and decreasing the burden of regulation. As a result, the financial sector in many developing countries where it was largely publicly owned was itself rapidly privatized and deregulated. Many banks established links with foreign banks as a way of integrating with the international financial system. The greater international integration provided some additional access to resources and may have also made the financial systems more efficient in these countries but it simultaneously involved the banks in questionable activities like capital flight and tax avoidance. Hence, whether the overall impact on the economy has been positive must remain an open question. There is no doubt that new instruments and new services have become available to both savers and customers but, in the process, the size and activities of the financial sector have increased significantly relative to the rest of the economy even in the developing countries (Turner 2016). But, investment-GDP ratios remain roughly the same and output growth has not speeded up either in these countries, with the exception of East and Southeast Asia, and long-standing gaps in the sector, such as a shortage of long-term project finance or seed money for start-ups, remain as before (Genberg 2015).

Some General Observations

Against this broad background, two fairly obvious questions present themselves: *one*, given that most economies/countries have experienced a large expansion in the size of the financial sector what has society gained as a result on a cost–benefit ratio and *two*, what is now the relationship between the monetary and the real economy given that the latter is ostensibly less profitable than the former. As regards the first question, the Nobel laureate James Tobin attempted to answer it as far back as 1984 and others Andrew Haldane (2010), Hyman Minsky (1992) and Atif Mian and Sufi (2014) have also done it. All have come to the conclusion that in terms of the overall bargain for society financial services come at high cost and are poor value for money. Tobin's doubts were based on the fact that for financial services to deliver good value for money they needed to conform as closely as possible to the 'states of nature' imagined by Arrow and Debreu in which markets existed for all goods and services and for all maturities and contingencies and that all such markets had to be competitive to ensure equilibrium. In practice, given the high costs of providing the latter, financial markets have not, and indeed never will, be able to provide for all conceivable needs and maturities. Moreover, most economic sectors, including finance, have shown over the last three decades a strong tendency towards concentration and cartelization. In other words, finance provides not only a limited part of the states of nature of Arrow and Debreu but the sector itself operates sub-optimally as a quasi-monopoly. Neither finance nor the other markets/sectors in the economy can therefore achieve or promote optimality.

Haldane has argued that the apparently high profitability of the sector is a mirage as it rests on largely arbitrary values of the assets being traded and, given the resources at their disposal, these values can be easily manipulated by those doing the trading. Minsky postulated that the vast expansion of the sector, far from progressively addressing any unmet needs of society for finance, would merely exacerbate the risks of over-leveraging in the economy especially in conditions of chronic uncertainty. Just as individuals and enterprises can overborrow, so can societies with systemic consequences for stability. Finally, Mian and Sufi maintain that financial services operate with an implicit guarantee against failure from the State. This not only condones but encourages and incentivizes risk-taking behaviour in the sector and risk-taking in finance facilitates the exploitation of the public by rent-seeking. It should also be stressed that overall financial sector risks are of an entirely different and much higher order of magnitude compared, say, to the limited impact of fluctuations in agricultural production or even the bankruptcy of an individual manufacturing enterprise might have on the economy. Taking all these caveats and doubts together the real value of financial services, as currently organized, to society is questionable.

As regards the second question, it has been known that there was a sharp distinction between the 'real' and 'monetary' components of the economy. And this was brought into stark focus in the 2007/08 financial crisis. Traditionally, the real economy referred to the production of goods and some services whereas the monetary component referred to prices, their rate of change, interest rates and the cost of intermediation. The classical quantity theory of money stated that, broadly speaking, an increase in the supply of money would raise the average price level in the short term. Keynes' contended that moderating price increases by controlling the quantity of money was not realistically possible and once inflationary expectations had set in—such as because of a poor harvest or other supply shock—the State had no ability to limit an increase in the velocity of circulation and thus in the quantity of money.

Keynes did believe that the interest rate as set by the central bank was a useful instrument in pricing and hence controlling its supply but it tended to work in an asymmetrical fashion. It was easier to expand money supply by reducing the interest rate than to reduce it by raising the rate. Therefore, its effectiveness as a means of monetary control was limited. In this respect Keynes' view was that obtaining an ideal or 'optimal' balance between overall supply and demand in the economy and, hence, a stable price level was not compatible with a free market system as markets failed from time to time leading to periods of under- or over-utilization of the factors of production. Given the likelihood of market failure the State would almost certainly have to intervene in the economy, especially in periods of high unemployment and weak demand. What role then could the financial sector play surrounded by such uncertainty?

All of the above are important qualifications and they collectively would have a close bearing on the true importance of the financial sector in an economy. There is almost no argument that the importance of finance has been exaggerated, especially during the last three decades in the media and has come at major cost to society. Today, given the change in the overall climate of opinion following the 2007/08 financial crisis it is feasible, indeed necessary, to look to the future and to plan for a radically reformed financial sector that conforms more closely to the needs of society. It is self-evident that there should be greater stability in its operations. In addition, it should not be a vehicle for the self-aggrandizement by tiny elites who work in the sector and their wealthy clients who make use of its services.

The remaining chapters in the book will seek to build the argument that a major effort to fundamentally reform the sector is needed. As with efforts to deal with the problems posed by climate change, parallel efforts will have to be organized at the national level within an international plan of action. It will not be easy and doubters and naysayers will be aplenty, especially those with an intimate stake in the current arrangements. Indeed, the likelihood of strong opposition to such an effort should be presumed. But, first the intellectual argument has to be won.

References

Foroohar, R. (2016). *Makers and Takers: How Wall Street Destroyed Main Street*. New York: Crown Publishing Group.

Genberg, H. (2015, December). Capital Market Development and Emergence of Institutional Investors in the Asia-Pacific Region. *UN ESCAP Asia-Pacific Development Journal, 22*, 1–32.

Haldane, A. (2010). The Contribution of the Financial Sector: Miracle or Mirage. In Part of a Co-authored Chapter *The Future of Finance*, LSE Report, London.

Kay, J. (2015). *Other People's Money: Masters of the Universe or Servants of the People*. London: Profile Books.

Lazonick, W. (2010). Innovative Business Models and Varieties of Capitalism: Financialization of the US Corporation. *Business History Review, 84*(4), 675–702.

Mian, A., & Sufi, A. (2014). *House of Debt: How They Caused the Great Recession and How We Can Prevent It from Happening Again*. Chicago: University of Chicago Press.

Minsky, H. (1992). *The Financial Stability Hypothesis* (Working Paper 74). Annadale-on-Hudson, NY: Levy Economics Institute.

Pettifor, A. (2017). *The Production of Money: How to Break the Power of Bankers*. London: Verso.

Silver, N. (2017). *Finance, Society and Sustainability: How to Make the Financial System Work for the Economy, People and Planet*. London: Palgrave Macmillan.

Turner, A. (2016). *Between Debt and the Devil: Money, Credit, and Fixing Global Finance*. Princeton: Princeton University Press.

CHAPTER 2

Money, the Real Economy and Financial Services

Abstract This chapter states that Keynes, Minsky, Tobin and others warned about the dangers of too large a financial sector and in this context money, of which bank credit is a large part, impacts on the real economy and vice versa. Too much money will affect the price level and will reduce the ability of relative prices to perform their signalling function for investors. However, the ability of central banks to affect changes in the money supply or to control the cost of production by varying interest rates has been found to be asymmetric; that is, lower interest rates might boost activity in the economy but higher interest rates cannot deflate asset bubbles. Since the 1980s, as the sector has been deregulated risk-taking has multiplied. Furthermore, increasing financialization has brought additional risks of default and of over-leveraging in the economy to the fore.

Keywords Economic growth and development (O11)
Financial regulation (G18) · Modern monetary theory (E31)
Monetary policy (E52) · Capital markets (D53)

Historical Background

One of the central problems of both classical and modern economic theory is the relationship between money and the real economy, i.e. the production of actual goods and services and the role of banks as

S. Ahmed, *Ruling or Serving Society?*,
https://doi.org/10.1007/978-3-030-00521-4_2

creators of money and facilitators of transactions in that regard. For a considerable period in the nineteenth century and until the advent of the Keynesian revolution, the production of goods was analyzed purely in real terms; it was only in the 1930s that the monetary system was recognized as a critical element within the economy with an intimate bearing not just on the general price level but through its influence on relative prices on the quantities in which goods and services would be produced and as a measure of profitability.

Monetary theory attempts to link the determination of prices with demand, supply and costs, including the cost of money. It also examines the functions of money and the role of banks within it and addresses issues like inflation, i.e. the speed at which the value of money is declining, the level of unemployment and exchange and interest rate fluctuations. Monetary practice is embodied in the framework of policies and regulations whereby society, through one of its agencies, the central bank, attempts, first, to preserve the value of money and, second, provides incentives to invest in the production of goods and services so that adequate supplies of these goods are available to the public. It is worth stressing here that no good or service will be produced if it does not generate a profit, i.e. surplus over costs. Within an enterprise, questions of cross-subsidization are likely to influence the precise quantities in which particular goods will be produced but such decisions are still bound up with profitability, in this case the long-term profitability of the enterprise as a whole.

The system of relative prices is an elaborate signalling system in an economy through which the myriad choices of consumers are aggregated and balanced. The decisions of producers determine the supply of a good or service; the decisions of consumers determine its demand. The interactions of supply and demand determine its price. Changes in prices and the response to these changes in the aggregate, determines the way society allocates its productive resources. When an increase in demand is more than the increase in supply prices go up. When this happens, new enterprises move into the production of the good or service concerned. The opposite happens when demand for a good or service declines. Price movements are thus signals that link the preferences of consumers with the decisions of producers. In addition, prices play a rationing role by eliminating some of the extra demand when they go up and some of the extra supply when they go down thus bringing supply and demand into balance, albeit with a time lag. The relationship between money and the real economy is embodied in a branch of Economics called monetary theory and practice.

Seen in historical perspective, as soon as the production of things became part of a complex division of labour in society and barter ended, paper money became not only the medium of exchange but enabled society to measure the relative values of labour, land and all the other values locked up in the wide variety of assets that constituted its capital. The classical economists had felt that money was no more than a medium of exchange, but it was clearly more than that. Whatever money was not spent on immediate consumption and was saved was also potentially an asset. Before paper money became widespread, society had used gold and silver coins as money. This was because the two precious metals were physically durable, had a limited supply and were therefore useful and acceptable as stores of value. The original money which consisted of such coins could in theory be issued by anyone, anywhere as gold and silver were universally acceptable. But when bankers or others issued paper IOUs in excess of their holdings of gold and silver, they had created a completely new asset. Its value, however, depended on their reputations. This asset, therefore, came with a problem. There was no physical constraint on how much of it could be issued, and this meant that if too much was issued, it could lead to a loss of confidence in its usefulness as a store of value and ultimately become worthless.

In 1844, Britain had stepped into regulate the issue of paper money. The Bank Charter Act of that year placed a statutory limit on the amount of paper money that could be issued that was not backed by gold or silver, and restrictions were placed on the issue of paper money by institutions other than the Bank of England (these were abolished in 1921). This was done so that paper money could play the role of a medium of exchange and a store of value at the same time. However, if it was going to be the latter, then it must not lose its value by too much of it being in circulation. What all this indicates is that while money possesses multifarious attributes, it is not good as a *measure of value over time*. If it has been issued in excess of the production of goods in any given period, it will begin to lose its value and cause inflation.[1] Hence, if paper money is to play its dual role, its issuance needs to be monitored and controlled.

[1]There have been several instances of price increases of 20% or more annually at the time of the second Oil Shock as, indeed, of hyper-inflation in post-World War I Germany.

This is a stylized description of the traditional relationship between money and the real economy. Over the last three decades, financial services have moved away from their traditional intermediary role and have become heavily involved in the securities markets with a much sharper focus on short-term profits. As long ago as 1931, the UK set up the Macmillan Committee on Finance and Industry to look into the relationship between the real economy and the financial sector. This Committee, in which Keynes played a major part, sought to understand the mechanics of financing trade and industry in the economy in the wake of the Great Depression of 1929. It concluded that while the Depression had been driven by a collapse in the stock markets subsequent actions by the authorities had failed to rebuild overall confidence and most productive enterprises had complained of a chronic difficulty in accessing finance for investment as opposed to the short-term working capital needs of enterprises. As a result, post-depression recovery had been slow and patchy. In fact, the lack of finance was a major factor in the inability of the UK to rebuild its manufacturing base and this was almost certainly a factor in the lack of preparedness of the UK when World War II began in 1939 (Roll 1962).

Again in 1959, almost 15 years after the end of World War II but only five years after the end of rationing, the slowness of the post-war recovery of the UK economy vis-à-vis West Germany (as it was known at the time) and Japan and the inability of UK manufacturing to narrow the productivity gap with the USA led to another committee being established to analyze the on-going problems faced by UK manufacturers insofar as they related to accessing finance. The Radcliffe Committee on the Working of the Monetary System was constituted in 1959 with a wide-ranging brief to recommend measures to improve the performance of the economy. It concluded that financial services operated with a very short-term time horizon, and while there were a variety of institutions to cater to the needs of the manufacturers in the monetary system in the area of share issuance, very few truly understood the particular longer-term needs of a manufacturing enterprise, especially one that might be described today as an Small or Medium Enterprise (SME). The Committee felt that the monetary system as a whole was more comfortable in financing domestic and foreign trade and in providing expertise for share issues in which money could be made quickly and with little or no risk than in supporting new enterprises over the medium to long term, say, in the development of new technology as in Germany.

These weaknesses remained into the 1980s and with the Big Bang in 1986 were effectively formalized. The main responsibility of finance then became increasingly bound up with the issuance and trading of securities and in promoting fee-earning M and A activity.

However, trading in securities has little, if any, relevance for the real economy, and even M and A activity is often undertaken for tax reasons. Proponents of securities markets believe that they assist in the price discovery process of both existing and new shares and bonds and they therefore play an important role in the capital allocation function. Indeed, this modus operandi and predilection of the finance sector has been adopted by large sections of the real economy as well, i.e. a preoccupation with short-term profits and it is that which influences capital allocation more than any other measure. It is important to understand the impact of the latter on the overall monetary environment within which the real economy has to function.

Monetary Economics in Practice: Extracting the Surplus

Apart from a limited number of individuals who might be genuinely happy with their lot, the majority of people aim to better the material circumstances in which they live and achieve a standard of living that is above that of mere subsistence and to do so steadily year after year. In the ancient world and, indeed, even in the first 150 years or so of capitalism, say, from 1750 to 1900, only a small minority had the ability to satisfy such ambitions. Between 1900 and 1950, the world had to endure two world wars and one massive depression that radically altered not just the structure of the global economy in the form of vast losses of capital and huge civilian and military deaths but also the intellectual climate of opinion. The latter was driven by capitalism's inability to prevent huge booms followed by busts that threw millions into destitution in the 1930s. From 1950 to 1975, driven by a more egalitarian, social democratic view of society, the global economy was characterized by rapid economic growth and development. This enabled the hitherto improbable ambitions of economic security and social prosperity to be fulfilled virtually across the world. Large numbers of people, including some of the very poor in the developing countries, experienced unprecedented improvement in their standards of living. The greatest successes were witnessed, however, in the developed countries, but some developing countries also made substantial progress as global trade growth was translated into global growth in jobs and opportunities. But taken together, progress over the last 60 years or so still leaves only about half the world's population living moderately comfortable lives while for the rest life is a struggle. About 20% of the world's population remains poor, having to survive on less than $2.50 a day. At either end of the income scale, the differences are enormous and have no rational explanation. The top 1% have command over half of global wealth while four-fifths have limited incomes and own no marketable assets (Oxfam 2017).

These figures mask similarly uncomfortable truths in individual countries. While developing countries naturally have proportionally more of the poor in their populations, even the richest countries still have significant numbers of the poor, around 12–15% of the population.[2] The most pertinent detail in the distribution of wealth globally and in individual countries, however, is that today the rich are becoming richer everywhere while the incomes of the poor, although perhaps not becoming lower, are stagnating. The relevant question therefore is how the wealthy have succeeded in becoming even wealthier than before over the last three decades. This cannot be explained away as the inexorable working of a system over which society has no control. Fundamentally, it can only be explained as a failure of political economy; in the way, the financial sector and the real economy have been allowed to evolve during this period at the political level.

Although political economists from Adam Smith onwards have attempted to understand how the rewards accruing to society through the joint efforts of land, labour and capital arise and are shared, there has never been a satisfactory explanation as to why the surplus value so created ends up almost in its entirety with the owners of land—in the case of agricultural produce or with the owners of capital—in the case of an output from a factory. Utilitarians like John Stuart Mill simply hoped that in the end, all would be well and that fairness would prevail. It was Karl Marx, however, who has provided the most cogent explanation. Marx explained that in both slave and feudal societies, the manner in which surplus value was extracted and then captured by the slave-owner or feudal lord was self-evident; the serfs and slaves had no political rights and were, in fact, legally barred from even attempting to exercise them. In a modern economy, the same process is hidden within a series of tacit

[2]The UNDP Human Development Report provides much relevant information on the global distribution of wealth as do NGOs like Oxfam.

'agreements' between capital and labour. The latter is still exploited by the former by appropriating the major part of surplus value that it produces. This surplus value is the equivalent of gross profits. Marx had conceded that labour was not entitled to the full value of this profit as the profit had also to pay for the wear and tear of the capital equipment being used and to pay interest on any sums borrowed as working capital. In fact, if labour took the whole of the surplus value there would be little or no capital accumulation (Robinson 1966).

In the arrangements that have evolved since the beginning of the twentieth century, it is the owners of capital who still capture the lion's share of the surplus. Between 1950 and 1980, the balance of power briefly shifted a little against capital through redistributive tax measures taken by governments and by the role that trade unions were allowed to play a role but the influence of both has declined since then. There is thus a fundamental problem in the way rewards are distributed in an economy organized along capitalist lines. Under capitalism, those who control the means of production do not own a specific resource; they exercise control by virtue of their command of finance represented by the ownership of shares. In other words, the power of the owners of capital is measured by their financial wealth and investing in the production of goods and services is effectively a means towards its greater accumulation.

In Marx's scheme of things, as true in the twenty-first century as in the nineteenth and twentieth centuries, the overriding motivation in an economy based on the private ownership of capital is command over finance that, in turn, facilitates its accumulation by maximizing the surplus. This can be done by controlling costs, especially labour, but now including R and D and, more recently, contributions to employer-funded health care and pensions. By explaining this relationship, Marx provided the intellectual means to analyze not just an economy in 'static equilibrium' but of the drivers of growth, i.e. the 'dynamic equilibrium' of capital accumulation and of the distribution of the surplus value between labour and capital and how the latter was able to expropriate the surplus value. We can also understand now that all decisions by the owners of capital presuppose that the money in an economy will keep a stable value and that they will be allowed to exploit whatever opportunities for investment that they can identify. It falls to the State via its institutions to ensure that these conditions are met and that the State will accordingly give priority to achieving price stability and by providing the appropriate legal environment for investors to maximize their surplus towards these ends.

The Price Level and Inflation

As soon as labour was accepted as being integral in the production of goods and services, its costs came to occupy a central part of the discussion in Economics regarding price stability and the viability of investments, i.e. their ability to earn an adequate return. Price instability does not in itself impinge in a negative way on the decisions, or indeed, the profits of capitalists. But it does increase uncertainty, especially for the long-term future, and therefore reduce the ability of relative prices to provide reliable signals for investors in their decisions. Owners of capital thus expect governments to give priority to and to take action to ensure the stability of prices.

All those familiar with the political battles of the 1960s and 1970s, especially in the UK, will know that price stability and wages are intimately related. When modern capitalist production first emerged, labour was compensated either on a piece rate basis (cost of materials plus cost of labour time involved) on the basis of any skill that labour might have. Thus, the unskilled were given a subsistence wage while those with skills were able to earn an extra amount. Generally speaking, the level of wages is largely the result of historical accident with some skills compensated more than others and whether labour is available in abundance generally or in specific areas. With the passage of time, despite the use of labour-saving machines in many lines of production, wages became the main determinants of costs for any producer and the latter have looked to controlling them with the State getting involved in these efforts through incomes policies. Furthermore, relative wages could be varied by technology, but technology has to be paid for. The owners of enterprises have thus always attempted to vary the proportions in which capital and labour can be combined, but the process cannot be advanced in favour of capital indefinitely. Overall, while it has been in the interest of all producers that wages are kept low so that the surplus can be maximized, workers are also consumers and without their buying ability the markets for the capitalist's products would be curtailed.

A notable characteristic of wages over the years has been that they are easier to increase but difficult to reduce. Rising wages during booms can at least be partially offset by rising productivity but since wage rates cannot be reduced, producers can only sack, or temporarily lay-off, labour during downturns. Enterprise owners thus go to great lengths, especially over the last few years, to be able to have 'flexibility' in employment contracts and in any relevant legislation governing them.

When all factors of production are fully employed, it becomes difficult to obtain extra output if demand goes up. In these conditions, producers can raise prices and apart from any repercussions from a loss of international competitiveness the process can go on ad infinitum. Moreover, rising money wages for some groups of workers usually tend to put upward pressure on wages in the economy generally, and the uneven nature of technology can aggravate the situation further. The upshot has been that owners of capital regard the control of wages as essential to successful investment. They therefore expect the State to eschew policies like minimum wage legislation or high employer contributions for social security. Indeed, financial services have played an important, though indirect, role in facilitating the control and compression of wages. They have done this by providing labour with relatively easy access to loans, particularly over the last two decades. And by so doing, financial services have not only allowed the share of profits going to capital to increase but as indebtedness has increased have boosted their own earnings as well in the process.

The real influence on wages and on money and prices originates from the government's fiscal position. If the government is running a significant budget deficit it produces two effects: one, by borrowing from the existing stock of savings, it pre-empts their use by private investors; two, if it issues its own securities and monetizes its debts, it adds to money supply and risks causing inflation. Both phenomena put private investors at odds with the government. When Keynes first provided solutions to the problems associated with the trade cycle and talked about the importance of effective demand, he made budget deficits intellectually and politically acceptable. However, in little more than two generations from the 1970s neoliberal ideas had rendered the running of budget deficits essentially unacceptable. But, this was a temporary victory. In the aftermath of the 2007/08 financial crisis governments reluctantly had to conclude that in order to prevent a prolonged slump, there was no alternative to boosting effective demand except by increasing borrowing.

Money and the Process of Growth

Over the last two hundred years, the basic raison d'etre of investment has not changed. There are now stakeholders instead of shareholders, and corporate social responsibility has evolved to become more than a passing fad. But, the fundamental objective of investment is to earn a surplus. However, forms of organization have changed, and the old family-owned and family-run enterprise is less important than the mega-corporation whose operations straddle across borders and is not very different from a large government ministry. But success for both is measured by the surplus that they can earn, i.e. the profitability of their operations. In fact, the surplus is not just a measure of the success of the businesses concerned; it forms the income for a whole class of rentiers in the economy, all those who own shares in the enterprise. In some enterprises, maximizing the surplus may be tempered by a commitment to quality and technical excellence, or by investing in R and D or training employees in new skills, so that some of the surpluses may be reduced or compromised. But such aims, if pursued beyond some arbitrary point, often weaken its share price. This will, in turn, mean that the enterprise will not be able to raise finance if and when it needs it, however worthy its long-term prospects, a bizarre feature of the financial system.

Today, there are different ways that the power of finance manifests itself over the affairs of any given enterprise. An enterprise whose shares are underperforming will, in the short term, become subject to the 'shorting' of its shares. Over the long term, it may become subject to a takeover bid. In other words, the value of an enterprise depends on how the market assesses its capacity to generate a surplus in the short term; the enterprise itself and whatever it might do to boost its longevity is of no importance. In fact, its long-term prospects by investing in R and D are likely to be treated with indifference. Finance holds all the cards. Indeed, in today's world even national loyalties are no longer particularly important. Patriotism can, and does, influence the standing of an enterprise in the eyes of its stakeholders and may influence the behaviour of its management but earning a surplus *in the short term* is the key. A startling statistic from the USA and UK suggests that compared to the 1970s the proportion of profits distributed to shareholders had roughly trebled by 2010 (Foroohar 2016). This phenomenon is particularly visible in the financial sector but applies, more or less, to the entirety of the corporate sector in the developed countries. As a result, the former has had to resort to riskier behaviour to preserve its overall profitability, while in non-financial enterprises critical R and D investments have been underfunded.

These attitudes are particularly evident in the USA and UK where the short-term performance of a company's stock is how its management is going to be judged. As profitability has become higher in finance, even non-financial enterprises in these countries have set up financial operations mostly for the securities markets. This represents the growing importance of financialization in the developed economies. Indeed, in the case of General Electric in the USA, the size of its financial operations had become so large by 2013 that the Financial Stability Oversight Council of the US government classified it as a 'systemically important financial institution'. In other words, it had become a bank in the eyes of the US government. Unsurprisingly, this blurring of the lines of demarcation between manufacturing and financial enterprises has delivered few, if any, demonstrable benefits to the wider economy, for instance, in the form higher investment levels. On the contrary, the increasing interconnectedness of finance and of the real economy has greatly increased the likelihood of the impact of any difficulties being rapidly transmitted across the sectors in these economies.

The Neoliberal Revival in the 1980s and Its Aftermath

These trends have to be seen, too, against the background of the surge of neoliberal ideas since the 1980s. But, in order to understand developments in finance since the 1980s a brief excursion into the evolution of capitalism would be useful. Capitalism, Economics and finance have had a chequered history since the former emerged as the dominant framework for the economy in the eighteenth century and the latter developed as a separate intellectual discipline to explain how the former worked. Propelled by the spate of new inventions in the nineteenth century-capitalism in the beginning was primarily about making things. This phase was followed by the growth of domestic and international trade and the need to finance it. Financial services of increasing complexity thus emerged and grew to support manufacturing and trade and, indeed, over time replaced usurious moneylenders. Economics had very little to say about the role of finance in the economy until the latter years of the nineteenth century. Prior to this, Adam Smith's *Wealth of Nations* and Ricardo's *Principles* had laid the basis of political economy in which relationships between citizens, between citizens and the State and between States, rather than theological precepts, became the foundations of social enquiry.

Within political economy conflicting ideas about the individual and the State were embodied in the very different views of Thomas Hobbes and John Locke even before Smith and Ricardo came on the scene. Hobbes had stressed individualism and self-interest while Locke had emphasized the importance of consent on the part of those who came under the authority of the State. But together, they represented the beginnings of utilitarianism and of modern political economy. The subsequent development of the overall economy and of industrial society in the nineteenth century created additional intellectual and political challenges. While industrial capitalism had resulted in an undreamed of expansion in the production of goods, for the wage labourer it had meant a life of hard toil not just for himself but for his wife and, very often, their children, with the ever-present danger of losing his/their jobs during downturns in the trade cycle. For the owners of enterprises, industrial society and capitalism had certainly been a revolution compared to feudalism. No longer was growth in trading or progress in manufacturing down to favours from the aristocracy or even the sovereign; it was down to the benefits from being members of a new mercantile class with its gilds, finance houses and cooperative endeavours. Moreover, this nascent secularization of society had awakened hopes that a new, somewhat less repressive age might be in the offing and political movements giving effect to these hopes appeared on the scene. The idea of fairness was born, and the study of Economics became the arena where the intellectual battles between the individualism of Hobbes and the gentler, more collectivist visions of Locke, and others, would now be fought. It was this social and intellectual environment that would influence how society and the economy developed in the future.

From the mid-nineteenth century onwards, the emergence of industrial capitalism and the associated need for finance led to the simultaneous establishment of banks, joint stock enterprises and the stock exchange. However, at the beginning, and for many years thereafter, only a small minority of the population made use of their services. For instance, only a tiny number of the population had bank accounts in Britain and France until well after World War I. Even after World War II, compared to today, finance was a fairly rudimentary activity primarily involved in providing short-term loans to enterprises that might be called working capital and small overdraft facilities to the better-off customers on the basis of the savings that the public had entrusted with the banks. A variety of other institutions also emerged at this time in which the less well off could put their small savings. In addition to the retail and savings banks, building and cooperative societies and the less visible merchant (or investment/wholesale) banks began operating in the City of London.

But, in the economy as a whole, finance remained the junior partner of those who made things and this remained true until the early years of the twentieth century. What dramatically changed perceptions and attitudes was the Great Depression of 1929 in which a stock market collapse led to a long-lasting global downturn with mass unemployment and bank failures. It is generally accepted that without the ideas of Keynes, partially implemented in the New Deal in the USA, the depression that ruined the lives of many millions of people, both rich and poor, would have lasted for many more years.

The New Deal and its associated growth in laws and regulations governing economic life, accompanied by an increase in government spending on rearmament prior to World War II eventually ended the Great Depression. Intellectually, classical Economics had signally failed in as much as it had not been able to provide the needed solutions for the problems in the economy that the Great Depression had brought to the fore. It was the Keynesian revolution with its interventionist ideas that had showed the way. Nevertheless, Economics would remain divided into two ideological approaches, laissez-faire and interventionist, and that division continues to this day.

In the immediate aftermath of World War II, interventionist ideas embodied in the Keynesian revolution became *de rigueur* virtually across the world and during these years they enjoyed an intellectual primacy equal to that of Adam Smith and Ricardo. In fact, that primacy remained unchallenged until the mid-1970s. For Keynes, the Great Depression of 1929 had been a major learning experience and it led him almost directly to a reappraisal of the role of the State, both in preventing such events in the future and, if they occurred, to render them as brief and as harmless as possible. The creation of the welfare state was a natural consequence of what is now known as the Keynesian revolution. With the benefit of hindsight, the three decades or so from 1945 to 1975 are often described as the apogee of capitalism characterized by high growth, low unemployment and price stability, the latter coming to an end only with the first Oil Shock of 1973.

The factors that contributed to this golden age are many and are disputed to this day. However, high government spending in the economy on infrastructure, social protection, free public goods provided by the State and public expenditure on research and development played a major role. A conducive international environment based on a rare degree of agreement between nations in the post-1945 world, and the creation of multilateral organizations like the United Nations, World Bank, IMF and GATT also contributed. But, even the latter were a manifestation of the belief that the State could intervene in the economy in order not just to tackle the instability of the trade cycle but to promote the collective welfare of society, in this case global society. The golden age was essentially a period in which making things, supported by efficiently delivered financial services to savers and investors, was still the primary economic activity. Economics itself, somewhat ambitiously, began introducing concepts from natural science in its work, such as general and partial equilibrium analysis. It began to advance the notion that the complex interrelationships in an economy could be mathematically visualized and subjected to appropriate policy interventions to deliver optimal socio-economic outcomes.

The golden age, however, began to run out of steam as inflationary pressures emerged. These were initially caused by the sharp increase in oil prices but the ground had been prepared by the persistent fiscal deficits run by the USA during the Vietnam war. In the USA, lower government spending on infrastructure and inflationary pressures caused growth to slow with significant knock-on effects on the global economy. This further undermined the ability of governments to continue to fund high public expenditures primarily through taxes. Now the school of non-interventionists in the economy was emboldened. They explicitly blamed public expenditures for the slowing growth and higher inflation. Inflation, for them, was primarily, if not exclusively, a monetary phenomenon and was the result of too much money, fed by the fiscal deficits, chasing too few goods. But, the solution for them was not action on the fiscal front, i.e. higher taxes to reduce the fiscal deficit. It focused instead on lower public spending and lower taxes. It also included a sharply reduced role for the State, the use of markets for resource-allocation and privatization of public assets. Laissez-faire ideas had thus returned and had contributed to the revival of what came to be known as the neoliberal creed (Ostry et al. 2016).

Finance, too, has been affected by this division between those who believe that it should be left to the markets and those who think that the State must intervene to protect the interests of those who use financial services. In the years before 1980, very much in response to the latter set of views, laws and regulations specifically for finance were passed as finance increased its importance in the economy as an intermediary between savers and investors and vis-à-vis other sectors. But, even by the late 1960s and early 1970s financial punditry remained a narrow specialism. Compared to today, a newspaper from the 1960s would only have a rather anodyne report on the stock market and little else.[3] The performance of financial services and the issues confronting them barely figured in these discussions as they do now. But, after 1980 an agenda of deregulation of finance was implemented with enthusiasm as neoliberal ideas advanced politically and belief in markets and market-based outcomes was promoted vigorously while well-founded doubts about its efficacy were pushed into the background.

In the event, however, neoliberal, laissez-faire solutions have not worked or at least not worked for society as a whole. Vast riches have been made by the owners of capital, facilitated by the stock markets and financial services, at the expense of labour and, indeed, of all others who do not own shares or do not have access to financial services. Moreover, over three decades or more growth has remained subdued, and lower taxes have not led to massive new productive investment but have worsened the fiscal position. Meanwhile, unemployment has remained high except in those economies that have been successful in creating a host of low-paying jobs. Over the last 30 years or so virtually, all governments, including conservatively oriented ones like Germany,[4] have become massively indebted in both the public and private realms. But, above all, the implementation of neoliberal ideas at the political level has brought greater inequality and lower social cohesion and created some of the most difficult challenges for societies and governments across the world.

Financialization Marches on

How did financial services evolve in this new climate of opinion? Up to the late 1970s, finance was not only regulated by a panoply of laws and regulations but financial services themselves attached great importance to their fiduciary obligations. From the 1980s onwards, non-intervention now combined with globalization, Western financial companies were impressively agile in recycling the growing surpluses of the oil-producing

[3]The *Financial Times* and the *Wall Street Journal* were founded in 1888 and 1889, respectively, but catered to a tiny readership.

[4]In the case of Germany, it is necessary to point out that following the reunification of West and East Germany in 1990, the former has spent around $1 trillion on all the costs associated with reunification.

economies—inflated after the second Oil Shock of 1979/1980—in the form of sovereign loans to a small group of developing economies. Many looked upon these developments as presaging a globally integrated economy in which global savings would help fund economic growth and generate prosperity across the world.

But, within less than three years this optimism had morphed into the developing countries debt crisis of the 1980s. Banks had recycled the surplus oil revenues to the more developed low-income countries on the assumption that the States cannot go bankrupt. What their thinking had ignored was that while the States, unlike corporate enterprise, do not cease to exist, they can become severely constrained in their ability to service their debts if their economic performance does not improve or if they cannot increase their foreign earnings commensurately. Within a matter of a few years exactly that scenario had come to pass. The second Oil Shock caused a severe global economic downturn, and none of the heavily borrowed countries could service their debts. A number of developing countries, primarily in Latin America but also in Asia and Africa, thus had to turn to the multilateral institutions, mainly the IMF, to find a way out.

The way out provided by the IMF was highly conditional. Intervention would now take a back seat, and the IMF would wholeheartedly implement the ideas of the non-interventionists. The indebted countries would have to follow strict structural adjustment programmes, and these programmes were the mirror image of what had happened in the developed countries: reduced government involvement in the economy, privatization of the public sector and a liberalized, deregulated economy. Thus, by the mid-1980s virtually the entire world, except the Soviet bloc and East Asia, was implementing policies and programmes—with varying degrees of enthusiasm—that fell under the thrall of neoliberalism. A few years later, as the Berlin Wall fell and the Soviet Union and the Soviet bloc disintegrated, the victory of the non-interventionists appeared to be complete. But, as ideological triumphalism collided with reality, it soon gave a new twist to the tale.

In the 1980s, the USA had raised interest rates to very high levels in order to squeeze out inflation. This had produced dangerous repercussions not just in the USA itself, in the form of the Savings and Loan Association failure (FDIC 2002),[5] but had indirectly led

[5]The Saving and Loan Associations of the USA were thrift associations, the US equivalent of UK building societies. Between 1986 and 1995, 1043 out of 3234 went bankrupt and their depositors had to repaid by the Federal Government.

to the developing countries' debt problems. Thus, far from reducing uncertainty and instability the resort to marketization and increased financial integration had the opposite effect in the global markets. Moreover, with a liberalized and deregulated financial sector operating with fewer checks and balances, huge volumes of funds began to flow into the equity and bond markets creating the first of the stock market bubbles. What had happened was that financial markets were not responding to a sober analysis of the so-called fundamentals (demand conditions in the sector, quality of corporate management, quality of the workforce, development and infusion of new technology); they were being driven primarily by the random judgements and reckless behaviour of market speculators in the securities area and stock markets across the world were marching upwards with highly paid financial analysts providing the intellectual support for these phenomena.

It turned out, however, that this type of financial intermediation was not based on 'science', i.e. on a rational cause–effect of the relevant trends. It was based on the vagaries of human biases, and it soon became obvious that market operators had failed to subject their ideas either to rigorous criticism or their decisions to genuine stress-testing.[6] Hence, contrary to the views of the neoliberals, financial markets were not found to be efficient trading and pricing platforms for the real economy but merely facilitated highly skewed decisions and, sometimes, the corrupt practices of market operators. Herd instinct and irrational exuberance had taken over markets, and markets had become prone to major errors of judgement resulting in huge price fluctuations.[7]

Overall, therefore, a deregulated financial sector has provided opportunities galore for speculation in the new environment. Massive volumes of securities have made markets more volatile. In other words, large sums of money can be made with only tiny price fluctuations in the underlying securities. It has marked the coming of age of financialization. Some old-fashioned lending still takes place, but the primary focus of financial sector operations from the point of view of profit-maximizing

[6] A lot of the stress tests are not unlike the scandals in which pupils of some schools were told the questions in the exam papers before they sat them.

[7] The collective wisdom of markets is often assumed to be infallible. In practice, it is no more than the views of like-minded men and women who bounce their ideas within a narrow circle of friends and colleagues and result in herd behaviour.

behaviour now centres round speculating in the financial markets. In 1988, to assuage their critics international banks had come up with the first Basel Accord regarding the need for a minimum level of capital vis-à-vis assets so that risk could be contained.[8] But, as subsequent crises have shown, the Accord has had little effect as far as risk-taking in the sector is concerned.

Over the last three decades, the wholesale/investment banking arms of the retail banks have not only expanded speculation in the markets to an extraordinary level but invented many esoteric instruments for the purpose. The new instruments, based on the securitization of millions of loans, are technically supposed to widen access to financial markets while at the same time reducing risk for investors. But, experience has shown that securitization merely shifts and nebulizes risk; it does not make it go away or even make it cheaper to insure against it. And credit rating agencies have been complicit in creating a fog of unreality in the financial markets by giving consistently high ratings to these new instruments. Moreover, since they can be bundled to provide higher returns than normal loans, investors and speculators have been ready to underestimate the risks involved and have thus found them to be attractive investments.

Thus, these instruments have indirectly widened the range of opportunities for speculative behaviour in the financial markets to an astonishing degree. Derivatives markets, for example, are close to $700 trillion (in terms of outstanding value) as against global GDP of $75 trillion. In the USA and UK, the ratio of financial assets to GDP is between five and seven times (Turner 2016). While conventional textbooks have always sung the praises of financial deepening, these orders of magnitude are clearly excessive. That is not all—activity in the sector has become highly concentrated. Finance today has all the characteristics of a cartel, and cartels enable rent-seeking to flourish.

This is not what the ideas of the non-interventionists had promised or visualized. In their ideal world, deregulation was meant to increase competition, lower costs and incentivize the sector to come up with new instruments to manage and minimize risk more efficiently and improve

[8]The Basel Concordat of 1988 agreed at the Bank for International Settlements in Basel was the first time that the concept of capital adequacy, i.e. capital as a ratio to assets became operational in banking.

allocative efficiency. In the process, assets would be more realistically priced, there would be no more, or significantly fewer, asset bubbles and the system as a whole would be an efficient intermediary between savers and investors. Indeed, even the regulators had bought into the desirability of leaving things to the markets. But, what came instead as the new reality of liberalized markets unfolded was the complete opposite: increasing complexity of the instruments being traded, increasing price volatility driven by speculation, the creation and intensification of asset bubbles on account of herd behaviour and the extraordinary interconnectedness of the various institutions, both retail and wholesale, in the markets leading to an unprecedented degree of vulnerability of the entire system to a single adverse event.

That is not all. Two other negative characteristics that have emerged as a direct result of the evolution of the financial sector are also worthy of note. As financial market activity has expanded and the internal reward system has become increasingly tilted towards short-term performance, it has significantly affected priorities and behaviour in non-financial enterprises as well. The shrinking time horizon of decision-making has already been alluded to. This has made enterprises desperate for short-term profits at the cost of enhancing the long-term competitiveness of the economy in which they function. Globalization has made the manufacture of low-quality products and economizing on the development of worker skills and morale common across the world. In the developed world, takeovers and share buy-backs has become a prominent feature of corporate behaviour in recent years, especially in the USA and UK, a feature actively encouraged, in turn, by investment banks for whom it has generated welcome additional revenue at no risk. There is little doubt that these characteristics have made the financial system fundamentally unstable with serious implications for the rest of the economy (Turner 2016).

It could be argued that not all the problems discussed here can be laid at the door of the financial sector itself. Better targeted regulation should be able to deal with errant behaviour by penalizing it where and when it occurs. Indeed, it could be further argued that as the real value of financial services ultimately lies in their ability to deliver efficient intermediation between savers and investors, plus a payments system that minimizes transaction costs in the economy, only efficient institutions can and should be able to thrive. But, here too, any objective assessment raises many doubts. For instance, the payments system is over-dependent on IT technology and this technology has a habit of breaking down.[9] In addition, there was a genuine fear during the 2007/08 crisis that the failure of a single bank might well have triggered the entire network of banks and others to seize up at major cost to the economy. The effects on ordinary people of such an event are not hard to imagine.

In an ideal world, the sector should be able to cater to all conceivable demands for loans and for all conceivable maturities. But, in fact, unless the regulator steps in, in all market-driven systems financial services tend to favour particular sectors more than others. In the UK, for example, the largest deployment of loans is in the property sector. Lending to non-financial enterprises constitutes less than a fifth of all loans (Kay 2015). This happens because lending against property is considered less risky, and even international regulation, such as the Basel accords, is biased in that way in that it systemically overestimates the value of property, whether for lending against or as collateral. As said elsewhere, one of the components of regulation is the capital ratio, i.e. the amount of capital that a bank needs to keep in relation to its assets and this ratio plays a vital role in the bank's profitability. If loans to a particular activity are considered more risky, the bank has to hold more capital. Property is considered the least risky of all activities. It consequently gets the lion's share of loans from the banking system. But, by doing so, banks generate immense upward pressure on prices in the entire property sector, especially in markets where there are institutional supply constraints such as the UK. Once such biases get built in, they can always be blamed on the judgments of all-knowing markets—based on the mantra of 'you cannot second guess the markets'—letting serious economic and social problems to emerge and to fester.[10] In such a scenario, financial sector profits turn into negative externalities for society.

The role of wholesale/investment banks in the intermediation process is particularly problematic today. These banks do not take retail deposits from customers but operate on lines of credit from the retail banks or with the funds deployed with them in their role as fund managers. With these funds, they participate in the securities markets. In addition, they acquire huge resources for their extensive wealth management operations

[9] Trustee Saving Bank (TSB) in the UK being its latest example.

[10] It is a moot point whether the collapse of manufacturing in the Anglo-Saxon economies has been a cause or an effect of the lack of support from finance. The direction of causation is difficult to establish in this case, so it could be both.

in which they provide a range of services to the wealthy. Taking the two together, investment banks have grown far bigger than their retail counterparts. Moreover, their forte lies in creating and trading in newfangled investment instruments like CDOs, derivatives, high-frequency trading, spoofing and so on and in M and A activity. Trading in these instruments and in the markets appears to be a relatively riskless source of substantial revenue streams for the institutions concerned; their usefulness to the wider economy can only be guessed. Similarly, even in M and A activity mergers have been followed by demergers and, more frequently, by asset stripping. The impact of their activities thus has significant backward and forward linkages, and they effectively impinge on the entire economy.

Financial Services and the Securities Markets

What then can be said about the larger rationale and impact of financial sector activities in the securities markets, the activities that are most in the public eye and are the most discussed in the media? In the USA and UK, financial services, although possessing enormous institutional depth and resources, consider the provision of support to enterprises for investment purposes as a secondary activity. The financial sector does help enterprises with IPOs and bond issues, but these are, in the context of the large balance sheets in the sector, a relatively minor sideshow. Their main activity of issuing and trading securities and doing so in increasingly bizarre ways is of little help to the real economy. The counter argument is that as financial sector evolution has been market-driven and markets represent the collective desires of myriad savers and investors there is nothing odd in this. But, the question arises: can it really be the case that a market-driven system is there merely to promote speculation in the securities markets? One example should serve to shed light on how this has happened and the bizarre, if not perverse, nature of its activities for the rest of the economy.

Elsewhere in the book, the increasing complexity of the instruments created for speculation in the securities markets has been mentioned. The bizarre nature of some of the trading instruments and practices vis-à-vis the latter, such as synthetic derivatives and spoofing, is worth mentioning. It might be useful to look at another similarly bizarre practice that has developed in these markets over the years. This practice is trading the Volatility Index (VIX), a creation of the Chicago Board Options Exchange (CBOE). The VIX is designed to measure how investors view different levels of fluctuations in share prices, both up and down; in terms of the hedging they would be willing to do to protect themselves against major downward movements. In other words, buying and selling hedging instruments themselves in sufficient volumes can modify the index which would then give a completely artificial measure of the actual underlying volatility of the share prices.

This is akin to saying that if enough people insured themselves against a particular event the likelihood of that event occurring would be reduced, not that the cost of insurance would come down. As far as share prices are concerned, although the relationship might be contrived, it is not beyond the realms of possibility that if enough hedging instruments were bought against their downward movement would be reduced. But, share prices are affected by a whole range of unpredictable factors, both natural phenomena like earthquakes and floods and unnatural ones like conflicts and political turmoil. Indeed, the largely predictable 2007/08 financial crisis was not predicted by VIX. To imagine therefore that trading in VIX serves any useful purpose for the real economy, or even for the financial sector, is beyond belief. It does not reduce risk—its claimed virtue—and it produces no information regarding the prices of the underlying securities on which it is constructed. While it certainly generates profits for the sector, it does so by what can only be described as gambling in the securities markets.

What the discussion shows is that the banking system falls well and truly short of providing support to the real economy, especially for the long term. Trading in securities, many simply the bundling of mortgages and financing the buying, selling and renting of existing property, rather than in the construction of new units, makes little or no sense from a growth or equity perspective. Moreover, in the latter, market failure is widespread with private sector building enterprises rarely investing in housing at the lower end of the income scale. Here, as in other operations, the primary focus of the banks is to find ways of increasing their own revenue and larger, more expensive housing does that far better than smaller, less expensive housing. Thus, banks concentrate on those activities where the capital they need to hold against their exposure in the sector is low. In other words, making loans against property has already been built and indulging in numerous connected transactions but kept off balance sheet. This concentration means that the true function of banks now is effectively to extract rents from the economy rather than meet pressing economic or social needs. Indeed, the same happens when it comes to the management of savings including pensions. By and large, financial services provide a poor, high-cost service, characterized by high fees and a strong bias towards maximizing their own earnings rather than investing in improving the long-term performance of the economy.

Over the last two or three decades, it is also the case that the extraction of rents has created a dangerous moral climate in the finance sector and in the wider economy. Concentration on short-term profit maximization, a critical basis for the justification of entrepreneurial behaviour, is only a step away from manipulation and deception. Since the year 2000, there have been far too many instances of bad corporate practice, mostly in the banks. Just as responsible individuals, we are expected to observe not just laws but are also expected to respect prevailing social norms, corporate enterprises, too, are expected to behave in a similar fashion. But corporate behaviour falls well short of this simple standard.

The first set of incidents of malfeasance relate to the use of misleading information in order to gain a pecuniary advantage. This ranges from misreporting the annual profit and loss statements to mis-selling instruments/services to unwary customers. The second set of incidents of malfeasance relate to openly or covertly ignoring laws against accepting money without adequate checks as to origin and then hiding it away (money laundering) and helping individuals and enterprises avoid paying tax. So many banks have been caught indulging in these practices that their incidence cannot be explained away as minor or as the work of junior employees. It suggests more deep-seated issues and a wider malaise which betokens a casual attitude towards accepting the constraints of operating within the ethical framework in which individuals and corporate bodies have to exist if society is to function on the basis of trust. Since the answer to corporate malfeasance in finance is ever tighter regulation and more severe penalties, it indicates that the problem is perhaps more serious than the supporters of finance have been willing to concede. The danger of a wider breakdown in corporate behaviour—as others start to copy financial companies and match their profits and rewards in the form of bonuses to senior staff, is only too real.

Profit maximization is a worthy objective, but it needs to be pursued within the legal and ethical framework created for the purpose and in conformity with the norms of responsible behaviour. In this regard, malfeasance in the corporate world, and in banks in particular, has tended to occur far too frequently to be dismissed as the doings of a 'few bad apples'. In the early years of the Millennium, the succession of corporate scandals in the USA suggested that there was a serious problem affecting the corporate sector as a whole. Following the financial crisis, questionable behaviour in finance suggests that whatever solutions/penalties that society came up with ten years ago to confront the problem have proved to be entirely inadequate. It is a sad reality that far too many banks and investment companies have been caught breaking the law.[11]

The post-1980 deregulation of financial services has also had even more adverse long-term effects on social cohesion. In the economies where finance has been liberalized and deregulated the most, mainly the USA and UK, there has been a marked increase in inequality since 1980. Association is not causation, but without the contribution of the two most-cited culprits, globalization and deregulated finance, it is difficult to imagine how inequality could have reached the level that it has. The relationship between the liberalized availability of credit to the already well off and the steady rise in property prices cannot be wished away, and these causal connections have been provided by financial services. Likewise, the lack of access to credit at the lower end of incomes is also a fact of life. It is worth remembering, too, that such people also have less secure jobs and are therefore less likely to enter the credit markets anyway. In any case, financial companies exclude them as poor credit risks and they are then forced to rely on loan sharks.

Away from credit, the last 30 years have been marked by booming securities markets and there is no doubt that these markets have made possible the 'winner takes all phenomenon' that has characterized share issues in these markets. It could be argued that unlike the credit markets, stock markets are more 'democratic', i.e. that anyone with a commercially marketable idea can try his/her luck in them. But, stock markets in practice are not rational markets. They are prone to wildly unpredictable fluctuations. Hence, success in an IPO is not down to an evaluation of the company's business prospects but to the prevailing market sentiment which is strongly susceptible to herd behaviour. This does not suggest that decision-making in finance is characterized by a rational assessment of the underlying costs and benefits. The IT-related stock market boom and its subsequent collapse make stock markets a doubtful source of finance for new investors using or developing new technology.

[11]As of March 2017, the global banking industry had been fined $321 billion for offences ranging from money laundering to market manipulation. The figure is, however, only a tiny fraction of its assets.

Finally, the size of the sector and the amount of wealth that finance generates has enabled it to thwart any attempts to regulate its activities effectively. The problems of the 'revolving door' and of regulatory capture are two relatively anodyne ways of expressing a serious problem. An even more serious problem exists at the intellectual level. It is remarkable that despite all the scandals and evidence of malfeasance few economists and indeed, hardly any amongst the lay public in the USA and UK have really questioned the justification for the huge rewards that the financial sector gets. Indeed, having a large number of globally significant financial enterprises has generally been portrayed as a positive achievement and is considered a matter of pride for the countries concerned whatever the costs for the rest of society. These views belie the actual reality of the many financial crises that have occurred regularly since 1980 and the adverse consequences that have accompanied them for the general public.

Implications for Policy

What might be the implications of the preceding discussion for the conduct of monetary policy and for the regulation of the financial sector? The principal, if not the exclusive objective, of monetary policy is to ensure stability in the financial system. Price stability is, perhaps, the most important component of systemic stability followed by the level of activity in the overall economy. Apart from issuing statements on the desirability of particular events or courses of action, the central bank only has the interest rate at its disposal to influence what is happening in the financial sector. Here, the central bank's discount rate (the rate at which banks can obtain liquidity from it) can influence the full range of interest rates in the economy and thus the cost of credit. For instance, a reduction in short-term rates would make it worthwhile to borrow in order to buy securities offering a higher rate. This would raise the price of interest-bearing securities making shares more attractive. The converse would apply when short-term rates rose. In addition, the central bank could manipulate the money supply by buying and selling securities from the public, so influencing total bank deposits. Most of all, the central bank could alter the maturity structure of securities by increasing the volume of short-dated treasury paper to buy longer-dated and vice versa. Thus, on paper at least, the central bank has the power to influence both the structure of interest rates and overall liquidity in the economy to promote growth.

In real life, however, the power is asymmetric. A fall in demand could be offset by a reduction in interest rates and an inflation-producing boom could be countered by higher rates. Empirically, it has been seen that the interest rate is weakly correlated with both investment and consumption. Investment expenditures have long lead times and are normally financed with an enterprise's own funds. A small rise or fall in the rate of interest is unlikely to make a decisive difference to any proposed investment. Similarly, while marginally lower interest rates are likely to spur consumption expenditures marginally higher rates are unlikely to deter consumption significantly. Furthermore, in real-life situations in which asset bubbles have come into being, whether in property or stocks, the central bank has very little power to deflate them—however negative or harmful their long-term repercussions might be. A central bank can create and inflate an asset bubble; it has very little power to deflate it. It should also be noted that asset bubbles are politically popular, as they make some people very rich, and a central bank would be over-reaching itself if it attempted to deal with an asset bubble purely because of its putative long-term harmfulness for society.

From the perspective of the last three decades, one of the most important domestic influences of monetary policy on the real economy in a typical developed economy is the demand for housing. By and large, unless the situation is as dire as the current one prevailing in large parts of the world in which the ratio of average house prices to average incomes has doubled from 3.5 to over 7, as in the UK, what a family can afford in terms of servicing a mortgage depends very much on the rate of interest. Building houses, too, is very much influenced by the prevailing level of interest rates. Thus, in both instances, even small movements in interest rates can produce large effects on the demand for, and supply of, housing. But this is just one area of the economy, and in terms of its size relative to the size of financial services, it is unimportant.

Not so long ago, economists accepted the distinction between the real and monetary forces in an economy, although Keynes was never fully convinced that a central bank could achieve any but temporary stability with its power to manipulate interest rates and liquidity in the economy. It was the Chicago School, led by Milton Friedman, that elevated monetary policy to a level of effectiveness, vis-à-vis the goals of low and stable inflation and of low unemployment, that it had never actually possessed. Nowadays, not only has the distinction become blurry but bouts of instability have come and gone while central banks have looked on as spectators. The massive size and range of activities in the securities markets that now constitute financial services in which institutions can borrow and lend between themselves at a scale that no central bank can match has rendered obsolete notions such as 'lender of last resort'. And globalization has given financial services an ability to 'shop around' and indulge in regulatory arbitrage, i.e. seek out the most convenient jurisdictions for profit maximization. The implications for policy are that the real economy must now take a back seat while the needs of the financial sector determine the policies and priorities of governments.

A similar impasse in policymaking and economic theory had arisen in the 1930s. This was resolved by the ideas of Keynes whose diagnoses of the instability of capitalism were acted upon after World War II and laid the foundation of the long period of growth in the global economy, albeit unevenly distributed geographically and socially and across countries. Keynes showed that while monetary conditions and monetary policy formed a part of the whole economy they did not have an overriding pre-eminence in terms of their impact on the economy. The stability that markets demanded was achievable only through the maintenance of effective demand and low unemployment. But that does not mean that there is nothing else left to be done once high levels of employment have been reached and price stability prevails. The autonomous decisions of investors will not automatically sustain these conditions, and, as we have seen, long-term investments will be either neglected or eschewed altogether. Stable monetary conditions do not by themselves automatically lead to growth in the real economy.

Ultimately, it is the State that will therefore have to take steps to ensure that growth in the output of goods and services is firmly anchored in the economy and is *based on a socially sustainable matrix*. Today, the finance sector with its massive involvement in the securities markets has grown to a size that its view of the world takes precedence over the needs of society. Hyman Minsky, James Tobin and others had the foresight to warn that an overlarge financial sector, far from being a source of strength for the rest of the economy, could inflict real damage to it. The 2007/08 financial crisis has proved that their warnings were justified. It is for this reason that a fundamental rethinking of the role of finance is now needed. It is essential therefore to understand how exactly financial services have contributed to growth and development in the past. Radically reforming the sector to that is thus the central challenge and deserves the highest priority. In addition, an organized, well-thought-out and sustained strategy is needed to put finance under some form of democratic control where it can better respond to the needs of society, matters more fully discussed in the final chapter.

References

Foroohar, R. (2016). *Makers and Takers: How Wall Street Destroyed Main Street.* New York: Crown Publishing Group.

Kay, J. (2015). *Other People's Money: Masters of the Universe or Servants of the People.* London: Profile Books.

Ostry, J., Loungani, P., & Furceri, D. (2016, June). *"Neoliberalism: Oversold?" Finance and Development.* Washington, DC: IMF.

Oxfam. (2017). *An Economy for the 99 Per Cent.* London: Oxfam.

Robinson, J. (1966). *An Essay on Marxian Economics* (2nd ed.). London: Macmillan (1st edition published in 1942).

Roll, E. (1962). *A History of Economic Thought.* London: Faber and Faber.

Turner, A. (2016). *Between Debt and the Devil: Money, Credit, and Fixing Global Finance.* Princeton: Princeton University Press.

CHAPTER 3

Financial Services, Growth and Development

Abstract The chapter stresses that all economies need payments systems and liquidity to function. Development, however, requires long-term support for projects and start-ups and such support the financial system under-provides. Since the 1980s, banks have become preoccupied with lending to the property sector and capital markets tend to favour well-known business groups in raising finance. Meanwhile most large banks have shifted to the trading of securities whose contribution to growth and development is questionable. Similar trends are visible in the developing countries. In the process, rent-seeking and moral hazard issues have multiplied in both sets of countries. The case of the Bank of Credit and Commerce International (BCCI) (1972–1991) provides a salutary lesson in how otherwise well-meaning attempts at providing financial services in the developing countries can end painfully.

Keywords Efficient markets (O16) · Neoclassical finance (B13)
Price discovery (D61) · Risk-seeking (D53)

The Economy and Financial Services

All economies need financial services both for day-to-day needs as well as for longer-term investment; the latter presupposes the availability of long-term savings. Day-to-day needs are primarily for transactions for which liquidity and payments mechanisms have to be in place.

S. Ahmed, *Ruling or Serving Society?*,
https://doi.org/10.1007/978-3-030-00521-4_3

Somewhat longer-term needs are for domestic and external trade in which transactions might take several months to be completed. Similar needs would arise in producing goods to order that entail the provision of working capital for raw materials and inventory. In the nineteenth century, the largest use of financial services was in domestic and external trade for which instruments like bills of exchange and letters of credit came into being. In the past and up to World War I such services were primarily provided by banks. Thereafter output growth and development generated long-term financial needs for capital investment. In the case of infrastructure and public goods, these needs were satisfied almost exclusively by the State raising resources through taxation; in the case of production by private investors they were satisfied, in addition to their own private funds, through the issue of shares and bonds in the stock and bond markets.[1]

As such needs became part of the normal, everyday life of a country's economy, institutions developed both to provide incentives for longer-term savings and to manage them. These were savings banks, building societies, pension funds and other fund management services. Financial services thus became an integral part of a modern economy. It should be remembered also that all economies also have a parallel informal or shadow financial system, more common in the developing economies of Asia than elsewhere, that contributes to the provision of finance in the economy. The informal system may not be large but by its very informality, less onerous documentation requirements and a lack of risk aversion probably plays a bigger role in many economies than is realized or given credit for. Near-usurious interest rates, however, would tend to reduce demand for its services.

In order to understand the true role that financial services have played, or currently play, in growth and development it is best to distinguish their role in a developed economy with mature institutions from a developing economy where incomes and savings are limited and institutions for intermediation are not fully developed. In many, if not most, of the latter category of countries the banking habit i.e. willingness to entrust any excess of earnings over immediate needs is still evolving. Most people prefer to keep whatever surplus funds they might have

[1] This is a somewhat stylized version of events. For instance, in both nineteenth-century Europe and the USA some of the initial investments in infrastructure were made by the private sector and some investments in production were made by the State.

in cash with themselves and most transactions are conducted in cash. In other words, Keynesian liquidity preference is high. As a result, even when such individuals do open bank accounts these are usually current or savings accounts with very short maturities. A preponderance of such accounts limits the ability of these institutions to make loans for any but the shortest of time spans. Hence, banks have ipso facto primarily been the providers of short-term, commercial banking services. Whenever longer-term loans are made the banks take on a maturity mismatch risk, i.e. between their assets (loans) and their liabilities (deposits). These risks have to be added to the normal credit risks emanating from customers/counterparties failing to honour their commitments and in external trade unexpected changes in exchange rates and political events. Banks in developing countries thus have to confront a complex array of risks in their operations and therefore operate with higher levels of liquidity than their counterparts in the developed countries. Parallel insurance and hedging instruments to mitigate risk have also come into being especially to facilitate transactions between parties who are unknown to each other. The range and cost of these instruments plays a major role in how efficiently trade takes place.

At the longer end of the time spectrum uncertainty increases in both developed and developing countries and for this reason the quality of decision-making on the part of investors takes on a critical role. Any country/society comes equipped with a set of strengths (factor endowments in the jargon of Economics) with which it will compete with others in the production of goods and services for the market place. But these strengths are not fixed forever. These strengths can be enhanced, such as by investing in infrastructure (roads, bridges, ports, flood control and so on), by improving logistics and the productivity of land and by investing in education which enhances the skills and productive capacity of labour. Good quality decision-making is needed both on the part of the investors in order to identify the best and most profitable opportunities for investment that these strengths will make possible, and on the part of the savers to entrust their savings to the investors concerned. It is in this role that the intermediation process should, on the face of it, make its strongest contribution to development. In the following paragraphs, we examine whether this is, in fact, the case.

Development was once described as a process of capital accumulation, with financial services playing a central role in that process. But capital accumulation alone is not enough; it needs to be deployed to best effect, i.e. where it can generate the best long-term returns for the economy. Experience has shown that control over society's savings brings with it temptations to misuse them by dangerously under-estimating or ignoring risk or by skimming off through rent-seeking the value added created by others or by indulging in pointless speculation. These temptations exist in both developed and developing countries.

Financing Growth and Development

In deploying savings for long-term investment the biggest problem—in both developing and developed countries—is uncertainty about the future. In the 1950s, many developing and some developed countries attempted to overcome the problem of uncertainty through central planning in which the State laid out its long-term objectives and the means for attaining them. In centrally planned countries the plan was a rather inflexible system that not only tended to ignore or downplay the impact of unexpected events but also forced its principal components, productive enterprises, to adhere strictly to its discipline thus effectively killing off virtually all initiative. Neither savers nor enterprises had any freedom to experiment and financial services, such as they were, played a minimal decision-making role in how financial resources would be actually deployed. Indeed, they were no more than accounting entities. Other forms of planning that arose were of a more indicative nature in which only broad orders of magnitude for total spending in the public and private sectors of the economy were specified and financial services could play a more active role.

As it turned out, central planning, especially in its more rigid form, created more problems than it solved. Overcoming the combined uncertainties of demand for individual products or even sectors of the economy, domestic and foreign, and reconciling them with the pace of technological change and the domestic and global macroeconomic situation proved impossible for a central agency despite the use of sophisticated mathematical techniques. Even by reducing macroeconomic stability to general guidelines it was next to impossible to ensure a sustainable balance between capital accumulation and consumption, between the material inputs required for the production of goods and the financial resources required, between different lines of production and between technology, productivity and wages.

Rigid planning, while it attempted to outline how the future might unfold and made theoretical sense, proved impossible to manage in practice. In real life, this form of planning involving the production of thousands of goods and services was associated with suppressed inflation and shortages of even essential goods. Gradually, planning lost its appeal and even in centrally planned countries there was, first, a relaxation in the specification of physical targets and, second, converting plans to general estimates for the future on the basis of input–output tables. But, within the latter approach the State nevertheless continued to provide a long-term vision, backed up by not just policies but in the channelling of financial resources to support this vision. In the successful economies of East and Southeast Asia planning was not abandoned completely but replaced by industrial policy on roughly the same lines as Japan had done in the 1950s under the aegis of the Ministry of International Trade and Industry (MITI).[2] Moreover, the system of planning allowed countries to identify a sustainable growth trajectory for the country, to understand how the resource constraint for such a trajectory would be overcome, to develop a long-term relationship between the public and private sectors of the economy and for the State to invest in public goods and infrastructure.

Industrial Policy

What industrial policy seeks to do is to set out a path for a country's long-term development that centres round the promotion of particular industries either in the context of import-substitution or export-promotion. In terms of growth and development financial services thus have a clear notion of how the State collectively views the future on behalf of society. Hence, taking a long-term view of how the economy might evolve over the next 10–15 years becomes easier and financial services can become more fully involved in the development of the economy. If there is no industrial policy to guide them, as is the case in most developed countries, financial services, given the uncertainty, either cannot, or do not have the ability or, indeed, an incentive to take a long-term view of the economy. They proceed instead to operate on the basis of

[2] The planning regimes of, say, Malaysia and Thailand, were much less rigid than those of China and Vietnam which were centrally planned economies and were also less rigid than the planning system of South Korea.

maximizing their short-term profits and concentrate on those sectors/activities that support such profits.

As already stated elsewhere, the short-termism of financial services not only damages the economies concerned by neglecting sectors with a higher long-term growth potential, it has encouraged wasteful rent-seeking in the securities markets and in several developed countries, in the frenetic buying, selling and renting of property. Even in the latter case financial services have not been fully *au fait* with the dangers posed by their own behaviour. For instance, overlending against property has almost certainly aggravated the wider problem of pro-cyclicality in the economy so that when the cyclical conditions become adverse it is finance that has to bear the costs of impaired values, a problem created by the finance sector itself. A number of other examples will further elucidate this criticism.

Over the last three decades as the time horizon for decision-making in finance has shortened, the institutional memory of the sector in how economies grow and evolve over the long term has been effectively and, perhaps, irretrievably lost. Very few senior managers in finance now have a critical understanding of how inter-sectoral relationships and value chains in economies are established, how new industries are created, how new markets are won and how technology interacts with existing skills. This is not to ignore the huge challenges that inequality will pose for the worst-affected societies for governance and how such economies are likely to perform, say, in improving total factor productivity in an environment of social polarization. The impact of global poverty and climate change are yet more serious challenges for corporate managers in the future. Simply ignoring them and concentrating on short-term profits may make decision-making easier but their impact on the long-term evolution of the global economy, and of many individual economies, cannot be wished away. This general indifference not only gives a peculiarly distorted view of the world in which the managers of financial services reside but encourages them to become even more casual in dealing with the uncertainty that surrounds them. At a practical level, it affects how they comprehend and assess risk. In addition, financial services devote significant resources in helping enterprises to maximize tax avoidance.

To put it in a nutshell, the principal job of financial services today is financial engineering, to get more and more profits out of existing operations, to encourage unnecessary M and A activity to earn fees and to convert equity into debt and vice versa, not for any valid growth reasons but as part of a strategy to boost its own earnings and/or for the enterprise to avoid taxes with little regard for its impact on the rest of society. But, doing so by ever more esoteric forms of speculation and/or by over-leveraging the entire economy does not suggest a high level of critical awareness of the environment in which it operates. For one thing, over-leveraging is not just counterproductive in principle, equally as it happens for individuals and for enterprises, but for the whole of society. For another, it means that the long-term investment needs of the real economy have been cast aside in favour of short-term profit maximization but which has then not delivered.

This has not been the situation everywhere. In analyzing the contribution of finance to growth and development two different models of successful intermediation in this regard have been Germany and South Korea, and it might be worthwhile to take a synoptic look at both countries, and some others, to understand how financial services have contributed to their success. Generally speaking, in both economies the short-term needs were more than adequately met and did not represent a weakness in the sector. The real difference that becomes apparent has been in delivering long-term support on a sustained basis. In Germany, compared to the USA and UK, the stock market does not have the kind of dominating role that an economy of Germany's size, depth and sophistication might otherwise suggest. As a proportion of GDP, Germany's stock market is less than half while it is more than 100% in both the USA and UK. Furthermore, although Germany is better known for its globally successful automobile and engineering companies, in terms of domestic employment its economy is dominated by SMEs or *Mittelstand*. These remain mostly family-owned enterprises but with close links with the public sector *Landesbanken* that have supported them in investing for the long term, in developing new technology, in finding new export markets and in allowing the managements of these enterprises to take a 10–15 year perspective in planning for their future.

South Korea, on the other hand, has been a laboratory (after Japan and MITI) of how industrial policy is implemented and how financial services are an integral component of such a policy. South Korea's industrial policy was developed and put into practice in the early 1960s by the military dictator, General Park. Within finance, banks played a crucial role, and it is important to stress that contrary to the neoliberal maxims of the 1980s the banking system was nationalized, not privatized, by General Park.[3] As South Korea embarked on an export-driven industrial strategy its first objective was to enter those fields of manufacturing in which Japan was becoming less internationally competitive, like textiles (including the manufacture of spinning and weaving machinery) and shipbuilding. The largest companies, the *Chaebol* were given ambitious targets for production and exports in these sectors, supported by an appropriate tariff structure and ample access to bank loans. But at the same time there were severe penalties for failure and some *Chaebol* did fall by the wayside when they could not deliver. And when they could not, others were quickly drafted into take their place. On the macroeconomic side, and almost uniquely in the history of development, high inflation was tolerated with courageous policies. While wages were adjusted upwards after a time lag, savers were protected by positive real interest rates and exporters by periodic devaluations with the won-dollar exchange rate declining from 600 to 1100 today. As a result, the economy always had a large pool of savings to draw upon, banks recycled these savings to the sectors earmarked by the government as part of its industrial strategy and exports always remained competitive as far as the exchange rate was concerned. South Korea is, however, currently faced with high levels of household indebtedness, a problem mainly created by lagging growth in wages. Notwithstanding their current difficulties, Germany and South Korea have been recognized as outstanding success stories in which the contribution of the financial sector has been significant in terms of long-term development.

Another, even more remarkable, success story has been the rapid development of China after the 1978 reforms. These reforms signalled a new openness to the outside world, a greater role for markets in the economy and an end to rigid centralized planning. The reforms also replicated some of the measures followed by Japan in the 1950s in terms of identifying industries that could form the core of an export drive and then supporting them with tariffs, bank credits and other measures. The openness that was the *sine qua non* of the 1978 reforms was conditional on the achievement of export targets which applied equally to domestic and foreign (usually joint ventures until the creation of the SEZs, the Special Economic Zones) enterprises. Finance was never a real constraint. China, then as now, had a very high savings rate, around 45% of GDP,

[3] It is important to stress this as neoliberals are ever-ready to take credit for the successful development experiences of East Asia.

with consumption compressed fairly strictly in the 1980s and into the 1990s, and the State-owned financial system was awash with liquidity. Nonetheless, the intermediation process was not all smooth sailing. In the second half of the 1990s banks had accumulated a significant volume of bad debts, primarily with SOEs (State Owned Enterprises), as over-capacity built up in some parts of the economy, and had to be recapitalized.

In the first decade of the new Millennium the Chinese government encouraged domestic savings to be channelled into housing and high-tech companies in IT via the banking system and away from industrial SOEs. This has resulted in an extraordinary surge in construction activity right across the country and a property boom in the tier-1 cities, Beijing, Shanghai, Shenzen and Guangzhou, with many individuals buying multiple properties on credit, probably for speculative purposes.[4] As a result, there have been oft-repeated warnings of a property crash and the banking system (especially its informal counterpart) left with a mass of non-performing loans. This danger has been a subject of discussion within and outside China for more than a decade but, while property prices have tended to ease, the worst-case scenario of a property crash leading to stressed bank balance sheets has so far not come to pass. On the plus side of the balance sheet China has seen the emergence of massive enterprises like Alibaba, Baidu and Tencent in the IT sector with the banking system and stock markets intimately involved in their spectacular growth.

In this context, it is worth mentioning, too, that the State in China can and does raise massive resources through taxation, through the ownership of SOEs, like banks, insurance companies, the cigarette monopoly to name only a few, and through the issue of debt instruments for the construction of large-scale infrastructure projects like the high-speed train and highways networks. Its position in the economy makes it by far the biggest player in the financial system. More uniquely, the State is both the creator and user of financial services; consequently it has been able to fashion the system not only to finance growth and development in the economy—partly through direct measures and partly through

[4]It is important to note that in the context of dire predictions of an imminent property and banking collapse in the country buying an apartment requires a hefty deposit, usually 30% of the purchase price, and mortgages whose term is rarely over 15 years, a markedly different picture to the situation in the USA or UK.

indirect policies, such as enabling private investment in housing—but to control and direct its institutional evolution. Both State and private companies have also used the stock markets to utilize long-term savings in the economy with some companies' market capitalization reaching the levels not far short of IT companies like Apple, Google, Facebook, Microsoft. While these remarkable achievements can be attributed in part to the huge size of the economy of China there is no doubt that they also speak of a successful partnership between the State, private investors and users of financial services that has enabled this to happen. Whether it can be replicated by other countries must remain an open question.

In South Asia, i.e. primarily India and Pakistan, both development and its financing have taken a different course. Both countries began with a formal system of planning and a mixture of publicly and privately owned financial institutions. But development did not pick up pace for the first three decades after independence because of a serious domestic resource constraint that prevented vital investment in physical infrastructure. In addition, the initial approach to development was based on import-substitution and the paucity of domestic resources was aggravated by a shortage of foreign earnings. There was thus a large premium on access to bank finance which became subject to political patronage and cronyism. Overall investment as a ratio to GDP never matched the levels that countries like South Korea and China have been able to achieve. Since the 1990s a more liberalized system has been adopted in the financial sector, especially in Pakistan where virtually the whole sector has been privatized, but this has not translated into larger resource flows in the economy for investment. Moreover, both countries run large fiscal deficits which are financed by borrowings from banks. Investment levels remain significantly lower than in East Asia and attempts at overcoming infrastructure investment constraints through public–private partnerships have not been successful. In India, for instance, the public sector banks are sitting on a large volume of non-performing loans with many public–private projects for which these loans were given either standing unfinished or suffering from massive cost over-runs and delays.

It needs to be re-emphasized that economic growth happens when the three factors of production, land, labour and capital, combine to produce an output in the most efficient way possible. In the past, and in the early stages of development, questions were not asked whether growth was happening by adding physical increments to the factors or by using them more efficiently. Nowadays, it is the latter type of growth that is preferred on the grounds of sustainability. If a country is a natural resource producer and is achieving high economic growth by using up its natural resources it is on an unsustainable growth trajectory, especially if it is an oil, gas or mineral producer. Even with renewable agricultural commodities, such as wheat, rice, palm oil and sugar cane, the test of sustainability is relevant since in the production of such crops countries might be misusing or over-using scarce water resources or indulging in over-cultivation leading to topsoil depletion as is the case over large parts of South Asia. Such practices would make growth unsustainable in the long run. More modern concerns now relate to the impact of growth on the environment and on CO_2 emissions. Above all, along with economic growth countries have to pay heed to development which is a broader concept that embraces the effects of growth on society, especially its distributional impact, and on more nebulous measures like equality of opportunity and social justice. How society collectively articulates its priorities in these areas, and the precise role that is given to finance, is a matter for the State to identify and implement. But, in the end it is the overall value and institutional backup that influences the different priorities that society has set out to give flesh and bones to its objectives of growth and development and how they will be achieved.

The Evolution of Financial Services in the Developing Countries: 1950–1975

For a considerable period of time after World War II the provision of financial services in the developing countries was almost exclusively in the hands of the developed countries, a reflection of the geopolitics of international finance, with US banks by far the largest and systemically most important. This was due not only to the fact that the USA was the largest economy in the world but US corporations with their extensive multinational operations were dominant in international trade and investment flows. UK and French banks and corporations came a distant second and third in the global pecking order. Against these formidable forces, some developing countries had one or two publicly owned banks but they operated almost exclusively in the domestic economy. Their foreign presence and operations were negligible. As for the others, even Japan remained a peripheral player on the global stage until well into the 1970s. At this time, in the developing countries, banks were needed primarily to assist with domestic and international trade while the longer-term funds for development would be provided by the State.

The idea that the financial sector could meaningfully intermediate between savers and investors in these economies was fanciful with gross banking assets amounting to no more than 10 or 15% of GDP. Gross savings, financial and non-financial, were also paltry, around 10% of GDP, in most economies as incomes had barely inched up after World War II. Other than raw material and commodity exports, external trade was heavily dominated by imports. In the domestic economy, the largest sector, agriculture, was characterized by subsistence farming and the rest of the economy consisted mainly of retail and wholesale trade and some small-scale manufacturing, usually food processing. Some countries had set up stock markets where private investors could notionally raise investment finance but this was primarily in the form of equity; debt finance was effectively unknown. Only well-established business houses risked forays into the stock markets. Thus, stock markets remained thin and trading volumes were small until the 1980s and they could be easily manipulated by stockbrokers and others. Overall, financial services played a secondary role to the State in financing development in the economies of most developing countries.

In the late 1950s and early 1960s, several developing countries had begun the process of setting up their own banks and these tended to be a mixture of publicly owned and private initiatives, the latter usually led by the principal business groups in the country.[5] The former included specialized banks for agriculture and industry and for foreign trade while the latter were often, but not always, confined to the main centres of business. The great bulk of the people had little, if any, access to financial services up to the 1970s. For both the publicly owned and private banks breaking into finance was problematic as it involved substantial upfront costs in setting up branch networks especially if it also involved establishing a minimal foreign presence, say, in London to compete with old-established banks such as HSBC, Standard Chartered and Grindlays when it came to trade finance. The lack of qualified and trained personnel to man the branch network was an added constraint. Financial services, including raising capital in the stock markets, thus made slow progress until the late 1960s.

[5] China has always had a publicly owned banking sector. South Korea nationalized banks in 1961 and privatized some of them in 1998. India nationalized its banks in 1969 and Pakistan in 1974 but the latter began to privatize them in the early 1990s.

This was the situation across much of Asia. In Southeast and South Asia banking was restricted to the ports and to the largest towns and cities. In East Asia, excluding Japan, banking had a varied history of fits and starts with colonial banks dominating foreign trade till after World War II. Thereafter, it grew mainly as a public sector activity with the State initially pushing it to cater to the needs of the rural economy. In Japan in the immediate aftermath of World War II and later in South Korea, financial services were extended to provide support for favoured industries and for exports.[6] Longer-term intermediation, for instance for pensions or for investment in infrastructure via the bond market, was rudimentary even in the more developed economies of Japan and South Korea.

The First Oil Shock and Financial Services in the Developing Countries

The situation changed qualitatively with the first Oil Shock of 1973/74, especially in South Asia. Now the oil-producing countries at least were no longer financially constrained from starting their own banks. They had the resources to compete with banks from the developed countries that were operating in these countries. The problem that oil-producing developing countries came up against, however, was not the lack of capital or deposits; it was what the new banks could do in terms of banking business to justify their existence. Being young, the banks had neither the experience nor the technical clout to compete with the major international banks. One area, however, was obvious, financing imports. Another area would be financing the construction of infrastructure and housing but beyond that the list of possible uses declined sharply. One solution that was found was to break free from the constraints of the domestic economy and to participate in joint ventures, sometimes in partnership with a well-known institution from a developed country. Such banks could then serve both domestic needs and establish an international presence and the latter would then not only be an outlet for business opportunities for investors from the countries concerned but play the role that the traditional banks of old had played: gather market intelligence for its customers, domestic and foreign, and provide trade finance.

[6]Japanese industrial development was choreographed by MITI and led to the emergence of the *Zaibatsu*. In South Korea, banks were nationalized by General Park and were used for the development of the *Chaebol*.

This was the model for the development of financial services that was broadly followed in post-1970 South Asia and in the Gulf with which South Asia had developed a close relationship through the export of manpower that needed banking services for home remittances. In East and Southeast Asia, on the other hand, the domestic economy was clearly the driving force and, other than Japan, few banks ventured abroad. A factor that deterred such forays was the informal entry barriers for such banks to establish themselves in places like London, New York and Hong Kong (then run by the UK).

In the mid-1970s, financial services began to make a mark in the developing economies. In East and Southeast Asia, where savings rates were high and tending higher, industrial policy and exports made increasing demands for finance that went beyond trade finance into what might be described as project finance. In South Asia, savings rates were lower but banks and stock markets began to play a more active role in financing corporate investments. In East and Southeast Asia banking expanded rapidly and supporting institutions like the stock market, stockbroking and quasi-investment houses also appeared and began to play a more significant part in private sector development. At the same time, especially in the early 1980s, developing countries, particularly in South Asia with their dependence on multilateral institutions such as the World Bank, IMF and ADB, came under pressure to liberalize and deregulate as part of the pro-market reform agenda that had become the conventional wisdom at this time. This followed other reforms that had already liberalized the balance of payments in the capital account, though not in the current account, exchange rates had been allowed to float and taxes were being lowered. There was a general feeling of optimism amongst the business community that the international integration of financial services would make capital-constrained development a thing of the past. Developing countries would henceforth be able to pursue their international comparative advantage to the fullest extent and become integral components in global production chains. Indeed, many global banks flocked to the developing countries for this purpose.

In the event, the neoliberal reform agenda made excessive demands on the institutional capacity of the developing countries. This was partly the fault of the sequencing of reforms in that it made no sense to liberalize the capital account before the current account of the balance of payments. This had already led to the debt crisis of the early 1980s. In addition, easier access to capital led to large inflows of capital that could not be effectively sanitized by their central banks, exchange rates appreciated and imports expanded as countries lost competitiveness. Balance of payments crises followed almost inevitably, especially in Latin America. Asian developing countries escaped relatively unscathed in the early 1980s with only the Philippines affected to a significant degree. Getting to grips with their debts involved many years of lost output growth, high unemployment and much social distress. In Latin America, Mexico succumbed again in 1992 and defaulted on its international obligations. Overwhelmingly, large US banks were involved in both crises.

The remarkable part of the international debt crisis is that the same events were repeated in the Asian banking crisis of 1997 with neither international nor US banks having learnt any lessons. This time, while Latin America was spared, South Korea, Thailand, Malaysia, Indonesia and the Philippines were again the most affected by their inability to service their huge external debts. Again, after several years of lost output growth and sharply increased unemployment, external debts were rescheduled, some small banks in these countries went under while others had to be nationalized. As a quid pro quo of the IMF-led rescue efforts the affected countries had to suppress public spending in order to reduce their budget deficits. Aided by a conducive international environment the Asian crisis was mercifully not long-lasting and driven by buoyant exports all the affected countries had returned to robust growth and a more sustainable external debt profile within a few years.

The striking lessons of both crises that emerged were, first, that the international institutional environment—the World Bank, the IMF and regional multilateral development banks would bend over backwards and save private banks from their acts of folly in making vast loans to these countries. Not only illiquid but even insolvent banks would be prevented from getting into difficulties. When it came to organizing the rescue measures on behalf of the affected countries the price would have to be paid by the people of these countries in terms of a substantial retrenchment in investment and jobs. The poor judgements of the banks that had made the loans went unpunished. It was a lesson that would not be lost on others in the wider banking community. It was realized that risk-taking could henceforth be undertaken without restraint. Second, international banking regulation, such as the capital-asset ratio, embodied in the Basel Concordat of 1988 (Basel I), that followed the Latin American debt crisis was never going to be enough. It is hardly surprising therefore that there has been a succession of agreements at the BIS in Basel, Basel II, Basel II.5 and Basel III. Given the rapid growth of financial services since 1990, there will almost certainly be the need for a Basel IV before too long. Moreover, a subsidiary and less appreciated lesson is that the problem in finance is not one that can be overcome with ever-stricter regulation. Deregulated finance has produced the reality of 'too big to fail' in the developed countries and while institutions might be smaller in the developing countries they pose the same generic problem for these countries. The problem essentially is one of perverse incentives made worse by the ever-present dangers of greed and hubris. In other words, as highlighted earlier, the reality is that senior managers have given unqualified priority to short-term profits and, in the process, their own careers have become inextricably intertwined with the achievement of unrealistic balance sheet growth and profit targets—a sure recipe for disaster.

The BCCI Scandal

Against this background, the establishment of the Bank of Credit and Commerce International (BCCI) and its demise in less than 20 years illustrates vividly what can go wrong in the finance sector even with the best intentions. Here, the motivation to establish it lacked a basic understanding of what financial services are ultimately for and why neither its management nor its regulators could prevent the rampant risk and rent-seeking that eventually undid the good that it was trying to do. The BCCI was a Pakistani-run but Abu Dhabi-owned bank established in 1972, initially also with Bank of America participation, and was incorporated in Luxembourg. It was closed by the joint action of regulators in the USA, UK and Europe in July 1991. By that date it had established a presence in over 70, mainly developing, countries and was particularly active in the useful provision of trade finance involving many developing countries in Asia and Africa. Despite the passage of time doubts still remain why the drastic step of closure was taken. In fact, in the light of the 2007/08 global banking crisis such doubts have only intensified as major banks have been seen to have behaved not just recklessly but also done many of the same unsavoury things that the BCCI was accused of doing. The question therefore arises: was the BCCI unjustly singled out by the regulatory authorities at the time? Indeed, the 2007/08 crisis, far more serious in its systemic ramifications than any before, has seen individual banks succumb to their own greed and incompetence but none has been forcibly shut down by its regulators, a punishment reserved only for the BCCI thus far.

Closing the BCCI was supposedly done in response to widespread allegations of malfeasance in the form of money laundering, bribery, false accounting, running a Ponzi scheme and, rather implausibly, if sections of the USA and UK media are to be believed, involvement in prostitution, blackmail and illicit arms deals. Moreover, some months after July 1991 it was the bank's US liquidator who voluntarily pleaded guilty on behalf of the now closed bank to serious charges in the USA. In other words, none of the allegations, other than those that arose from the entrapment of the Bank in Tampa, Florida in 1988 were ever substantively tested in any court in any jurisdiction.

But today, similar allegations of money laundering, facilitating tax avoidance and creative accounting have been credibly levelled against any number of major banks (HSBC and Wells Fargo are recent examples). Substantial fines have been imposed on several banks for doing these things; however, none have been closed and hardly any senior officer of any bank has been punished. As of March 2017 Bloomberg had counted well over 200 settlements between banks and regulators costing some $317 billion in fines.[7] Of the settlements already reached a small number of banks had been fined in excess of 10% of their market capitalization. However, not one bank has had its licence revoked.

It is worth noting the underlying ethos of the 1970s and 1980s was that the BCCI operated in a sector in which regulatory oversight was easily circumvented, especially by large banks operating with a plethora of subsidiaries and affiliates, a consequence of the deregulatory zeal of the neoliberals for the financial sector. Such banks also kept many activities off their books as many did in 2007/08 and probably still do today. Banking regulators often have to tread a fine line between strict oversight and creating panic if oversight finds that too many banks are operating imprudently. In fact, in most jurisdictions regulators are likely to bend over backwards to prevent even the whiff of panic, which is every regulator's nightmare.

It needs to be stressed, too, that for those who have followed the increasing financialization of Western economies since the 1980s in which not just banks but non-financial enterprises have become

[7] These fines may seem impressive but they constitute only a tiny proportion of their assets. In other words, they have been let off lightly.

financialized turning to the securities markets for a growing share of their profits while traditional core activities have taken a backseat, the 2007 crisis came as no surprise. Banking in most jurisdictions had succeeded in creating for itself a lax—so-called light touch—regulatory environment. However, this freedom from regulation had also facilitated the growth of an egregious culture in the modern world—in both developed and developing countries—of ever larger banks based on the self-serving notion of 'too big to fail'. This had merely entrenched excessive risk-taking as an acceptable business practice and the giving of massive salaries and bonuses to senior managers based on rent-seeking. With the benefit of hindsight we can see today that the BCCI was perhaps merely an unwitting exponent of extracting rents from the public in developing countries and from their migrant kith and kin in the developed ones through financial intermediation. A combination of incompetence and bad luck resulted in its business model becoming unstuck more quickly than might have happened in a more conducive environment with less media hostility. However, closing it down certainly contains more than a hint of spite when seen from the vantage point of 2017.

A more apposite observation is that when examined from a more macro perspective, light touch regulation has meant that banks in their pursuit of short-term profits have created a vast ocean of indebtedness over the last two or three decades through a systemic neglect of risk and indifference to their fiduciary obligations. Market discipline, the great panacea of free market ideologues, has had little impact on reckless behaviour either in the developed or in the developing countries. To rent-seeking has been added manipulation of markets and exploiting customers by mis-selling and over-charging them for products and services. Glaring recent examples are the Payment Protection Insurance (PPI) sold to unwary customers by British banks over several years and the charging of excessive fees by fund managers as damagingly brought to light in a study in 2016 on the asset management market by UKs Financial Conduct Authority (FCA). Similar scandals have occurred in the developing countries from time to time. While the incidence of such practices was beginning to be suspected in the 1980s, their existence now is taken as an unremarkable and accepted part of how financial institutions do business.

It is worth remembering that the BCCI, and other Middle East-based banks, were established to recycle the dollar earnings that flowed to OPEC members (for the BCCI, principally from Abu Dhabi) as oil production boomed in the late 1960s on the back of a buoyant global economy; recycling then received a major boost after the 1973–1974 oil shock. In this environment, the BCCI provided vital credit support to a footloose business community from the developing countries making its way out of Asia to the UK, Europe and North America and became active in cross-border trade and investments. Indeed, some of the unmet needs of a nascent but robust entrepreneurial business sector from the developing countries were catered to by the BCCI. But the Bank was embarrassingly inept in its operations, expanding its geographical coverage over-hastily and incurring losses in key business areas which it then sought to hide. Indeed, it might not be too far off the mark to aver that the bank with its penchant for creative accounting might have been only marginally profitable throughout its short life. Unsurprisingly, it had provoked critical scrutiny during much of its existence (e.g. the Senator Kerry enquiry in the USA and ever more rigorous central bank supervision in Europe) that further undermined its already poor reputation in the eyes of the public. Nonetheless, by the time of its closure it was in the top 300 of global banks by assets and one of the biggest private banks in the world, a considerable achievement for its Pakistani management. Moreover, while technically insolvent in July 1991, its Abu Dhabi shareholders were willing to restructure the bank and save it from collapse.

What then was BCCIs business model that ultimately proved its undoing? As far as one can tell what the BCCI actually did and, indeed, what proved to be fatal, can be best summarized under the rubric of more conventional issues in banking such as moral hazard and principal agency. Lacking a credible home base—having incorporated in Luxembourg and Cayman—and hence effectively functioning without access to a conventional lender of last resort, it had survived by unending deposit mobilization drives, by using excessively opaque accounting practices and by claiming the support of the deep pockets of its shareholders which most regulators simply accepted at face value. These practices were allied to a marked preference for relationship banking for building up the asset side of the balance sheet, a preference that bedevils banking in South Asia, especially in the private sector, even today. Risk-taking in the bank was thus rife and was encouraged by senior management to expand the Bank's balance sheet. It also included reckless and amateurish forays into the securities markets. But, whatever its internal management weaknesses and its flawed business model, neither its regulators nor its external auditors can seriously claim to have been unaware of what was going on in the bank.

It is, of course, unarguable that within banking, traditional functions such as short-term loans, guarantees, trade finance, domestic and international payments, seed money for projects and liquidity management are an essential part of a modern economy. However, over the recent past, mega dealmaking, trading in newfangled securities and wealth management have grown enormously in size. Globalization has blurred the distinction between domestic and international banking and cross-border financial services have, in turn, generated huge rewards for senior management in the process, often exceeding the dividends paid to shareholders. But, it needs to be emphasized that the rewards are based not on any recognizable notion of economic value addition. As pointed out earlier, in competitive markets factor earnings should ultimately correspond to some measurable notion of marginal net social productivity. But this is not the case in banking. Indeed, in banking, colossal rewards have accrued not to capital, i.e. the shareholders, but to senior managers. And, over the last few years, quantitative easing in the USA, UK and Europe—which is a subsidy from the public to the banks—has added further opportunities for senior managers to enrich themselves.

It has to be conceded that high rents can exist in any sector of the economy for periods of time when market distortions occur. In finance, high rents have been driven partly by high transaction costs in the sector; the transaction costs occurring because of the asymmetric nature of information between banking counterparties and the difficulties involved in properly assessing and pricing the risks involved, a problem that exists in both developed and developing countries. But, within the metrics of neoliberal finance many risks have been created by the banks themselves by building up huge portfolios of esoteric securities that are only traded between them on the basis of complex mathematical trading platforms. It is also well to remember that the sector is characterized by very high entry barriers, which has facilitated cartelization in the sector. These traits have also allowed questionable practices in the sector, including informal market manipulation and sweetheart deals, and have encouraged banks to indulge in increasingly bizarre activities, for instance, spoofing and flash trading, that have no relevance for the real economy and which the general public barely understands. Developing countries are less involved in the securities markets but boosting profits artificially through tailored buy-back agreements between institutions and sometimes even through bogus buying and selling transactions is hardly a fringe activity in many of these countries.

The implicit cartelization and the notion 'too big to fail' have sustained a delusion about the existence of supernormal profits in the sector and have driven the process of financialization in most developed and now increasingly in the developing economies. However, the high profits, real or imaginary, have generated serious principal agency issues in the sector. Remarkably, it is senior management that expropriates the rewards resulting from the unchecked risk-taking while the shareholders are left bereft. This expropriation has been made possible as banking operates with an indirect subsidy from the State and regulators are loth to intervene in the day-to-day management of the banks. Here, it would be interesting to compare the gross discrepancy in the pay and bonuses paid to the CEO of the State-owned State Bank of India ($35,000) with that of the CEO of similar-sized Bancorp in the USA ($11.6 million). The USA is roughly ten times richer than India and assuming the two CEOs perform broadly similar tasks the CEO of Bancorp is massively overpaid. Plainly, rent-seeking has been raised to a fine art in US banks.

In this regard, what is patently self-evident is that regulation has not been effective. At the national level, the failure has been on account of regulatory capture and 'revolving door' issues again affecting both developing and developed countries. Neither set of countries have been able to countenance closing down a bank on the grounds of reckless behaviour. There is also the questionable efficacy of the sensitivity tests that are supposed to inform the public about the risk profile of particular financial institutions. At the international level, negotiating Basel I, II and III have shown the extraordinary lobbying power of the financial sector whereby many, if not most, reform efforts have been successfully diluted.

Going back to 1991, the question today would be: did the closure of the BCCI signify any larger lessons with wider ramifications? By way of warning to the rest of the sector, hardly anything as the regulators who shut the BCCI themselves did not really understand, or wilfully ignored, the nature of rent-seeking in the banking industry. But, as stated elsewhere, the BCCI was probably an early, though clumsy, extractor of rent in providing banking services; its developing country antecedents made it an easy target for a hypercritical and hypocritical Western media. The latter did not help as it was always ready to assume the worst, more interested in scandalmongering than in trying to understand how virtually all financial companies extract rents from the rest of the economy and from the public. But, the latter have, by and large, got off scot-free.

Today, the striking reality is that a cavalier attitude to risk in financial services pervades this sector of the economy. Indeed, such an attitude represents to the outside world the most glaring feature of its vast operations and the notion *too big to fail* underpins the sector. The real risk today is not of illiquidity but of insolvency and saving such banks rests on the tacit assumption that governments (taxpayers) will always bail them out—indeed, bailouts are a form of rent paid by society for the privilege of having banks. The higher capital requirements of Basel III have yet to be tested in the context of a serious crisis. Moreover, across the world the traditional fiduciary function of banks exists in name only having been replaced by reckless behaviour across the whole industry.

There can be little doubt that financial services in the developing countries have been heavily influenced by the evolution of these services in the developed countries. The emphasis on short-term profits has incentivized risk-taking behaviour in the developing countries just as much as it has in the developed countries. Senior managers, already successfully scooping out rents through their conventional intermediation functions, have found new avenues to increase rent-seeking opportunities. Thus, many developing countries have added to their armoury of loans and advances with high markups, for instance, consumer loans. In some countries, they also operate in the capital markets with instruments that have been developed in the advanced countries, for instance, derivatives whose relevance for developing countries can only be guessed at. Thus, earnings have risen and the culture of giving massive rewards to senior managers has been transplanted in the developing countries with the same deleterious effects on the wider economies in these countries. Yet few in the developing countries have questioned or examined how and why this has happened.

As far as financial services are concerned, it can be argued that their role in growth and development today is largely superficial, especially in mature economies such as the USA and UK. While they intermediate between savers and investors, they are not primarily looking at and safeguarding the interests of the two but interjecting between them and pursuing their own interests. From a macro perspective, it is difficult to discern a strong link between the financial sector and the growth of the economy. Considerations of equitable growth are even less strong. Such judgements would signify an unsatisfactory state of affairs on their own.

However, with their ability to command society's savings financial services have not only the capacity to be indifferent to the its needs and, in the process, take a cavalier attitude to risk, but to multiply manifold the dangers of another financial breakdown to society. It is extraordinary that despite knowing these dangers many developing countries continue to regard the USA and UK financial sectors as models to be copied, a view that is all the more bizarre in view of their questionable role in promoting development but of their involvement in a major financial crisis roughly once every seven or eight years.

CHAPTER 4

Financial Services and the Crisis of Capitalism

Abstract This chapter observes that there is ample evidence of malfeasance both in finance and in the corporate sector of most capitalist economies in the world. Behavioural traits such as greed and hubris in finance are to the detriment of sustainable long-term growth. Another unwelcome development has been a reduction in the share of rewards going to labour in the distribution of added value by corporations in capitalist countries and these trends have aggravated the problem of inequality in many countries. In future, disruptive technology is likely to make these problems much worse and add both to social problems and to the uncertainties being generated by phenomena such as climate change. Senior managers of enterprises in financial services will have to confront a daunting array of issues in their work if they are to meaningfully support sustainable economic development.

Keywords Comparative economic systems (P51) · Economic ideologies (D63) · Social welfare model (L52)

Capitalism and Its Variants

Previous chapters have traced the evolution of financial services and their growing complexity since the 1980s. While financial services have grown in size they appear also to have moved away from their traditional function of intermediation between savers and investors. Many therefore

S. Ahmed, *Ruling or Serving Society?*,
https://doi.org/10.1007/978-3-030-00521-4_4

question the present utility of financial services, whatever their other merits, for the rest of the economy. Indeed, it would not be out of place to ask if the growing distance between the financial services of today and the real economy has played a part in the wider crisis of capitalism as brought to the fore by the 2007/08 financial crisis. Today, there is renewed and growing interest in how capitalism works, or at least its neoliberal version, and for the first time since before World War II serious questions are being asked about its shortcomings. It does not need saying that capitalism itself has many different variants, from the US way of doing things at one extreme with the Western European version of economies with large public sectors and high levels of welfare spending at the other. Amongst the developing countries, there are the bureaucratic capitalisms of the Indo-Pakistan subcontinent, the government-led hybrid economies of Southeast Asia and the special, if not unique, case of China. What all of them have in common, however, whatever the precise balance between the public and private sectors, is the belief that markets are useful adjuncts to the State in the allocation of resources.

In previously centrally planned economies like China this marks an important break with the past as the original objective of central planning was to plan investment, output and prices within a single, self-contained framework for the whole economy that would run for five years. Despite the acceptance of the role of markets in the allocation of resources, in some countries, primarily in East and Southeast Asia, belief in market-clearing mechanisms remains less than wholehearted. Their reservations are based on the fact that markets are prone to failure, especially in the provision of collective goods. In these countries, public or merit goods, such as education and health, have therefore remained in the public domain. In these countries, there has been a long-lasting consensus that governments acting on behalf of society can, and should, intervene wherever and whenever the situation demands, to improve outcomes if the objective of inclusive development is to be seriously pursued.

At a more fundamental level, however, there is more serious scepticism which arises from the highly skewed distribution of rewards between land, labour and capital in the production process under the market-based system and this critique actually goes back to the early days of capitalism even pre-dating Marx. Early economic theory indicated that these rewards were based on a 'quasi rational' market-determined distribution in as much as each factor was supposed to earn a compensation equal to its net social productivity.[1] But this was and remains capitalism's Achilles heel; in practice, rewards are massively skewed. The problem is that however rational the system of rewards might be in theory, none of the three factors are ever wholly satisfied with the way they are compensated for their contribution to producing an output, the lack of satisfaction being variously attributed at the political level either to too much, or too little, intervention by the State, with the views being determined largely by political or ideological biases. Capital, being by far the strongest of the three, has consistently argued for less State intervention as this tends to tilt the proportion of rewards in favour of labour.

In fact, more than 140 years after Marshall wrote his *Principles of Economics* and having seen the evolution of capitalism over this period, it is perfectly legitimate to say that how factors are rewarded is essentially down to an interplay of forces in which the intervention of human agency, along with the State, plays a major role. Market-clearing mechanisms come into play as a reflection of the distribution of political power in society and in the relevant institutions established for exercising it on the ground, as it were. It is worth stressing that markets are not, and have never been, the sole determinants of factor reward. For example, land rents in agriculture are primarily determined by the uneven quality of the soil, and more than that by the relative abundance or scarcity of land itself vis-à-vis the population and the availability of water. The latter is sometimes a gift of nature but is more likely today to be the result of investments, public and private, made over many years in the past for that purpose. In urban areas, land prices and rents, other than being determined by the prevailing land-labour ratio, are almost entirely the result of the application of the prevailing laws and regulations governing the use of land and both rents and prices can be altered by the stroke of a pen; in other words, human agency facilitated by the power of the State. In the case of capital, while its origins are national, it can be put to use anywhere in the world and, as such, it is always restricted in supply where it is needed most. Governments are thus eager to lure it with incentives, usually subsidies and tax holidays, to enable the needed investments to happen. As a result, capital can, and has always, earned a premium over its real productivity (Miller and Upadhyay 2000).

[1] By applying Samuelson's factor price equalization theorem, it is possible to visualize how each factor of production would be compensated in conditions of perfect competition.

But, it is an undeniable fact that it is labour that has the least power to alter the rewards that come its way. The price of labour, over and above subsistence, is the result of the level of education or skills it has acquired and neither can be changed over the short run. Furthermore, the options for labour are binary: either it can work or it can withdraw from the market and go on strike. Only in this way, can labour withhold its availability in the economy in the hope of raising its price. However, as would be self-evident, it cannot do so for long especially, as is the case, an individual worker is also obliged to care for his/her family and any others dependent on his/her earnings. Improving the relative level of compensation for labour, other than for short periods of time, has thus proved to be impossible. Thus, the share of labour in national income has remained stable or, as in recent years, declined in the developed countries.

This is where political economy comes in. All capitalist models, in the end, operate on the basis of the prevailing balance of political forces in any society. What has to be remembered, as said above, is that the rewards that the three factors of production receive are not the result of market mechanisms alone but the outcome of political processes made possible by the power of the State, and in the latter the three factors have unequal power, with labour the weakest of the three. This skewed distribution of power and rewards has been most visible in the USA where the share of labour in GDP has remained unchanged, or has come down, relative to the other factors despite rising productivity, while the share of capital has gone up. Much the same kind of phenomenon has been evident in other parts of the world but to a significantly smaller degree.[2] Yet, it is in the USA that belief in markets remains the greatest. It is hardly surprising therefore that inequality, a consequence of the skewed reward system, has increased across the world as it has been presented as the inexorable functioning of market forces. The striking feature of the incidence of inequality is that it has increased much more in countries like the USA and UK. What these two countries have in common is, first, they have accepted neoliberal ideas more enthusiastically than anywhere else and, second, perhaps coincidentally, in both countries financial services have grown massively in importance over the last three decades.

[2]In 2016, the incomes of 95% of US households were lower than in 2007. In the UK, real wages had fallen by 6% between 2009 and 2014.

It is unarguable that the recent history of capitalism is a history of politico-economic forces in action. Markets are more visible in all economies but this has been brought about by political action. The revolt against the Keynesian revolution that had delivered not just a remarkable recovery after World War II but the creation of the welfare state in Western Europe (though not in the USA) was only partially the intellectual victory of the technocratic arguments of the Chicago School. It was, in fact, driven more by the owners of capital, and supported by rentiers who controlled land and other assets, for a bigger share of the pie, the output or GDP produced by society. Assorted think tanks and research institutes joined in as unabashed cheerleaders. What the Chicago School proposed were measures to reduce the role of the State, to deregulate previously regulated sectors of the economy and to privatize publicly owned assets to free up the economy and thus 'undo' the harm that State intervention had done to the free play of market forces. The undoing was justified in the name of efficiency, no matter that it would favour capital. Led by influential organizations like the World Bank and IMF, similar policy prescriptions were then proposed to the developing countries under the rubric of structural adjustment programmes (SAPs). Here, too, they were accepted by the ruling elites with little or no questioning, partly because they were desperate for the help from these institutions but more because their interests were much more closely aligned with neoliberal ideas. Thus, both in the developed and developing countries the neoliberal agenda has been driven by special interests not just in the guise of science but by successfully masquerading as the promoters of the general good.

Impact of the 2007/08 Crisis

Today, however, a far less confident intellectual and political environment has emerged following the 2007/08 financial crisis. Up to about the mid-1970s, most economies had been run with a variety of restrictions on the freedom of capital on how it could be put to use. There were caps on interest rates, a separation of wholesale and retail banking and a variety of credit controls, most particularly on cross-border investments. But, after the first Oil Shock of 1973 and the huge expenditures by the US government on the Vietnam war the emergence of inflationary pressures and large global imbalances led to an uncertain investment environment and disenchantment with the way economies had been managed. In this situation, deregulation and the need to reduce the size of the government had a superficial allure and thus became irresistible policy objectives for most governments. The simultaneous progress of information technology meant that deregulation of financial services, especially in the area of risk management, could be achieved not just in theory but in practice. Between the mid-1980s and 2005, a period during which the Berlin Wall came down and the USSR collapsed, the global environment was one which confirmed that neoliberal ideas were the 'truth'. The euphoria of this period, however, ended abruptly in 2007.[3]

At the intellectual level, other than in some diehard think tanks, there is now an emerging consensus that neoliberalism has effectively had its day. It has failed to deliver the benefits that it was supposed to. Domestically, deregulation of markets and privatization has made no significant difference to economic performance in any country. Rates of growth continue as before or have declined and investment-GDP ratios remain unchanged or have declined. Indeed, even after a period of ultra-low interest rates under QE following the crisis, many eminent economists have concluded that the future is likely to be one of secular stagnation. Likewise with privatization, there is no evidence that there has been an upsurge in overall investment levels even in the privatized enterprises. Moreover, in the case of privatized utilities not only have prices gone up as rapidly as in the past, or more than in comparable unprivatized enterprises, the chorus of complaints from the public against poor service has risen to a crescendo—hardly surprising in view of their monopoly status.[4] Enthusiasm for yet more privatization of public sector enterprises or its UK version of Public-Finance Initiative (PFI) or of outsourcing of services previously provided by the State has therefore all but collapsed. Instability in financial markets continues as before. But, despite these failures, faith in deregulated finance remains stubbornly unaffected although it is here that neoliberal ideas have failed most, being as spectacularly wrong-footed by the crisis as ordinary people.

[3] Eric Hobsbawm compared the 2007/08 financial crisis to the fall of the Berlin Wall in 1989.

[4] The experience of the UK with respect to the privatized and non-privatized water companies is particularly apt. Since privatization prices have gone up the most in the privatized companies as have complaints from the public.

It should perhaps be re-emphasized that the financial meltdown of 2007/08 was not the result of war or natural disaster but emerged from profound flaws in neoliberalism itself. Neoliberal ideas reduced and over-simplified Economics precepts to a rough and ready framework that output and welfare gains would be automatically maximized if only market forces were allowed to work their magic. Enterprises would produce what was demanded while consumers would maximize their welfare by buying what they needed or wanted and would divide their income between consumption and savings according to their own preferences. Demand, supply, savings and investment would co-exist in near-perfect optimality as their magnitudes would be determined by the so-called wisdom of the markets. Not only that but in a globalized world economy conditions would be created that would lead to an efficient global division of labour and in due course, a matter of years rather than decades, the whole of global output would be produced in the most efficient way possible. This extraordinary view had completely ignored the reality of market failures in all economies in a wide variety of sectors, including factor markets. Moreover, the last half of the nineteenth century was a fairly close approximation to the ideal neoliberal world and while it did produce prosperity for a small number of economies in Europe and in North America, and here, too, on a starkly unequal basis, the rest of the world remained mired in poverty. But, there are other criticisms and objections too.

The first problem in neoliberal reasoning was to assume that not just individual countries but the whole world would be able to respond to the incentives that would flow from the lifting of regulations and other forms of constraints on the unfettered actions of investors in an identical fashion. Here, even if the widely varying levels of natural endowments and supply constraints in individual countries are ignored, neoliberalism does not sufficiently take into account the political and social context of different communities within countries, not to speak of the multifarious national identities and rivalries that straddle the world. Societies in only a minority of countries in the world live in a state of natural harmony; in fact, most countries are faced with regional and ethnic tensions that make their societies ill-equipped to take a view based purely on their collective interest. Political and economic decisions are heavily influenced by the way that the ruling class perceives the world and subsumes it within a larger narrative to protect and promote its own interests.

The second problem relates to the assumption that the full gamut of influences that determine economic and social outcomes in society are based on a rational analysis of the situation by rational investors and rational consumers who take rational decisions after gathering all the information needed for them. We know now that most people do not conform to this highly idealized rendition of how *Homo economicus* behaves. In fact, most consumers and most investors take a very short-term view of their utility or profit-maximizing time horizon and states with serious governments have to constantly grapple with the problems that such behaviour generates. An obvious example of this is adverse selection in saving for old age which very few societies in the world undertake to the extent needed, despite constant exhortations from the State and despite the reality of the experience of their own previous generations.

Capitalism and Inequality

A far more fundamental issue is that market-driven economies dominated by the private sector nearly always tend to deliver very unequal economic and social outcomes. This was true in the decades leading up to World War I virtually across the world and in the USA both after World War I and in the last three decades. After World War II, these tendencies were countered by the State through the use of redistributive social protection measures, as in Western Europe, or by the provision of good quality public goods, as in East and Southeast Asia. The post-2007/08 trends in the global economy have once again seen large increases in inequality almost everywhere. In Western Europe, and more specifically in the UK, redistribution has come up against budgetary constraints, some of them exaggerated for ideological reasons. But the budgetary constraints have arisen because, essentially driven by the media, there is an unfavourable public mood against higher government spending and therefore against higher taxes. In addition, following the 2007/08 crisis, a number of countries have found themselves in a precarious fiscal position after saving their financial systems from collapse and therefore find their freedom on the fiscal front significantly reduced. Now, ageing populations are also altering the arithmetic of redistribution adversely, for instance in the area of care for the elderly. At the same time, markets create winners and losers and the latter have to be protected by the State. But, if the State cannot raise the required resources to do so the whole of society has to confront the serious social, economic and political repercussions arising from this. The natural tendency, in such situations, is to find scapegoats and/or to take comfort in unrealistic populist remedies. Today, institutional capacity in most states, both developed and developing, is unequal to the task of confronting these problems.

The institutional capability in this context is not simply the existence of properly staffed ministries and agencies for this purpose. Institutional capacity in this context is that the responsibilities of the State should be to act as a fair arbiter, especially in the deployment of public resources on behalf of society. In most real-life situations, however, the ability of the State has been compromised: either it has fallen prey to strong sectional interests or it simply ignores minority concerns or, even worse, it has decided that the current arrangements are broadly acceptable and do not need any radical reform measures. For example, today, a higher tax burden on the well off simply cannot be implemented—a view that is based on bogus scientific grounds, a blatant case of ideology made to resemble objective reasoning. Hence, what institutional capacity really means is that society engages in an honest and frank debate on the issues rationally and then empowers the State to gather all relevant information and facts, including their different interpretations, to create a consensual climate of opinion in which it can play its role of a fair arbiter. However, in the UK and in several European countries, for example, neoliberal ideology reigns supreme. In the UK, austerity has been the centrepiece of economic policy for the better part of a decade. The apparent consensus in support of this has been achieved on grounds which have never been properly justified either by the organs of the State or in the research institutes or in the media, with a few notable exceptions. Austerity has been presented as entirely rational in the circumstances.

Of all the different politico-economic arrangements that exist in the world today by far the most striking is China's development since 1980 and its historical experience with total state control between 1950 and 1980. As a successful middle-income country, China's development has generated a significant intellectual challenge. Western commentators are upset that China calls itself a socialist country. As a result, admirers of capitalism have unilaterally decided to call it a capitalist country. It is important to remember, however, that its model for the economy, even today, is based on a central role for the State.[5] There is a large and growing private sector but the government has kept a tight rein on important sectors of the economy like finance, transport, communications and energy and on foreign investment and the country has thereby been able to avoid the major financial and economic upheavals that have plagued the rest of the world. China has, however, not been able to avoid the increase in inequality that has been a feature of the global economy over the last three decades.

Almost uniquely in the world, however, members of the ruling Communist Party have been dispatched to poor rural communities (for at least a year) as part of their training programmes. Moreover, throughout the last three decades as it has proceeded to deregulate its economy the key priority of the State has been the alleviation of poverty, not just expand the role of markets for its own sake. Rapid economic growth creating millions of jobs and generating ample fiscal space for the State has been used to implement wide-ranging reforms in health, education and social protection. Successive leaders of the Communist Party have been able to build a strong consensus around these policies with Party officials being selected for promotion according to their achievements in this area.[6]

Another facet of China's development that has been different to the rest of the world is how it has modified property rights after the 1978 reforms. All economists accept that China has combined deregulation without an accompanying headlong rush towards the private ownership of land and land-based assets, as took place in the USSR in the 1990s. Thus, land remains in the ownership of the State and agricultural plots are leased to farming families. These plots can be inherited but cannot be transferred to others except where they are resumed by the local county government for consolidation or for the construction of infrastructure or housing. In the latter case, the farming families are provided with alternatives or compensated in cash and encouraged/advised to start new businesses. Disputes have arisen about the level of compensation given

[5]The Chinese call their economic model either 'socialism with Chinese characteristics' or a 'socialist market economy'.

[6]The World Bank has estimated that the poverty rate fell from 85 to 15% between 1980 and 2005, equivalent to 600 million people, an achievement generally regarded as being without parallel in human history.

but in programmes involving millions of families, the incidence of such disputes has been negligible.

Town and Village Enterprises (TVEs) set up in the 1980s are another example of the prudence exercised by the Chinese State in the implementation of its post-1978 reform policies. TVEs were set up by local governments in partnership with entrepreneurs who were provided guarantees against unilateral action by their local government partners. These enterprises plus the ground rent from farm leaseholds provided local governments with the wherewithal to build infrastructure and deliver services such as education and health. A similar desire not to overturn long-standing arrangements in the country in a disruptive way motivated the State to protect the larger SOEs from the vagaries of global competition. As a result, special economic zones were set up from where foreign enterprises could operate and participate in the country's export drive, without affecting the operations of its own enterprises. These enterprises provided valuable templates for the country's fledgling private sector which now boasts of companies like Alibaba, Tencent and Baidu.

What lessons does China's development have for the rest of the world? In the most general terms and ignoring the undoubted importance of history and culture, whichever economic model, including Chinese socialism, is examined closely it is, at the end, some variant of a mixed economy, though with important differences. The neoliberal model, too, despite protestations to the contrary, relies on the power of the State to deliver the environment within which markets can flourish or even function properly and, in times of crisis, to provide the resources to allow recovery to take place. Similarly, the entirely laudable aim of equality of opportunity that all societies profess to believe in, will inevitably require large investments in decent education and health facilities. The trouble with the neoliberal world view is that it imagines a world that is only motivated by utility-maximizing individuals and enterprises whose behaviour is only modified to the extent that they have to operate through markets. In the ideal neoliberal world, therefore, you could leave virtually everything to the markets and they will deliver 'optimal' outcomes whether society finds them acceptable or not. In theory therefore, other than spending on the military and police, you would barely need the State. But the economic history of the world and the history of Economics from Adam Smith onwards reveal wide variations in human behaviour and these are, in turn, reflected in the way social science has built the theoretical foundations of choice in human behaviour.

Nearly all of human behaviour and its value system can be explained by the interplay of politics, economics and the metrics of the prevailing social contract. The one constant element in these arrangements is the institution of the State. Without the State, neither markets nor the elite would be able to function and the ability to exercise choice in daily life would not exist for society.

But, just as we must remain wary of the ability of markets to deliver optimal outcomes the State, too, must conform to minimal norms of effectiveness. Not just in history but many regions of the world today and not just in the developing world display widespread state failure. In the real world, therefore, states can be ineffective and corrupt and can be captured by sectional interests and they would, in those situations, do more harm than good. But States, failed or failing, cannot be wished away; nor can we deny the aspirations of all individuals, not just the rich, to be independent and self-sufficient, to lead their lives without the fear of ill-health for themselves and for their dependents and to be able fulfil their capabilities. Wise societies are those which can create the right balance between the responsibilities and capabilities of the State and the realistic aspirations of society so that the objectives of both social justice and of individual rights and aspirations can be achieved.

Can Technology Fix Capitalism?

As in the past, new challenges continue to arise in our lives that stretch our abilities to deal with them both individually and collectively as a society. One of the greatest challenges in recent history has been the continuing impact of rapidly evolving new technology, especially the Internet and IT. Over the last two centuries the development of steam power, the telephone and electricity dramatically transformed the physical environment in which the majority of the world's population had lived and made its living. These technologies, while benign in themselves, also created the phenomena of urban poverty and slums and it was only after many decades of struggle that the objective of social justice entered mainstream collective, political consciousness across the world. Social justice then delivered not only higher rates of growth and welfare; it became part of the global political consensus that led to the welfare States of Western Europe and the post-1950 model of inclusive development of East and Southeast Asia. Since the 1980s, the consensus has begun to fray, though not yet fatally. In this uncertain situation, many observers believe that technology will be able to solve the problems that are looming in the distance.

In order to discover what, if anything, technology can do to address the issues of insecurity, inequality and the profound feeling of despair amongst the excluded it is necessary to understand and keep more recent developments in capitalism in focus. Capitalism today is no longer dominated by steel and cars, as it was until the late 1980s, but by disembodied technology that exists in space and algorithms. Google, Amazon and Facebook sell products that have no physical shape.[7] These are the most valuable companies in the world and along with their Chinese counterparts in IT probably account for a massive proportion of global wealth, an extraordinary feature of today's phenomenon of economic and social inequality that transcends national borders. Moreover, this wealth does not exist in a particular location; hence, the relationships of its owners with society and with any state authority have become entirely nebulous. The owners and a significant number of their employees have become fabulously rich but these trends have bypassed entirely the hundreds of millions who use their technology and provide them with the data and information that they then sell to others. The impact of these technologies therefore has been to make inequality and exclusion worse, not better.[8] The new technology and the new companies exercise almost exclusive control not only of the 'space', physical and metaphysical, in which we the consumers of their services live, but they do not appear to be answerable and accountable to any higher authority. The unanswered question is: how will society make these companies follow a minimal code of ethics in their relations with society? It would seem, for now at least, that post-World War II experience based on the tenets of social democracy, such as public ownership, offers little guidance.

All disciplines that seek to explain either the physical or metaphysical world to us must be ready to be challenged. This is as true of natural as it is of social science. But, however provisional our knowledge and understanding of what is going on around us, the notion of an underlying morality should never be compromised. Over many Millennia of evolution, we have arrived at the objective of the 'collective good' that all societies are expected to strive for and to devise arrangements to that

[7]See Jonathan Haskell and Stian Westlake's *Capitalism without Capital.*

[8]And the future in which robots and AI are going to take over many tasks performed by humans is daunting.

end. Standards of individual and collective behaviour will be judged by how much they conform to some fundamental commitment to values such as trust, loyalty, consideration for others and a sense of fair play. In the teaching and practice of Economics, which influences so much of the way we comprehend the world, society seems to have reached a dangerous impasse. Since the 1980s, neoliberal beliefs have acquired the status of a quasi-religious creed and any evidence that might challenge it was until recently dismissed as the ranting of heretics. The 2007/08 crisis revealed that neoliberal ideas are unlikely to deliver socially stable outcomes but instead more insecurity in the form of poorly paid jobs and greater inequality. In this respect, the teaching of Economics itself, and of social science generally, will have to reflect the new uncertainty that now characterizes the role of markets and of the State in society. The practice of Economics in government, in the private sector and in research institutes is intimately bound up with the way it is taught and there are a number of pointers for what needs to go into Economics syllabi.

First, the world around us cannot be reduced to graphs and equations. Economics courses must begin with a study of our past that includes social anthropology to give a sense to students about how the societies of today became what they are. *Second*, economists should abandon their 'Physics envy'. Economics is only a science to the extent that it employs the tools of logic but its analyses are heavily dependent on assumptions. Some of these assumptions, such as utility-maximizing behaviour, do not, or only rarely, conform to reality. They need to be appropriately modified. *Third*, Economics must deal with the issues of how power is exercised in society and how it influences the distribution of both public and private resources. Marx, and political scientists before and after him, drew attention to the existence of a ruling class. Aversion to the name of Marx should not blind social scientists to the existence of such a class as an analytical entity and the effects it produces on society by its command of the levers of power and ability to dominate society not just politically but culturally as well. If democracy and the collective good are to have real significance in our lives then it is the duty of economists, and, indeed, all other social scientists, to tell the story as it is: to talk of rent-seeking, free-ridership and the manipulation of markets for private gain. Douglass North, the American Nobel Prize winner did not shy away from using psychology, sociology and politics to explain human behaviour and how all three had shaped the values of society and its politics. That is how we must re-learn Economics for the years ahead.

Reference

Miller, S. M., & Upadhyay, M. P. (2000, December). The Effects of Openness, Trade Orientation and Human Capital on Total Factor Productivity. *Journal of Development Economics, 63*, 399–423.

CHAPTER 5

The Future: Making Financial Services Subservient to the Needs of Society

Abstract Financial services need to be made subservient to the needs of society, to provide stable long-term support for vital projects with high social returns and to meet the needs of under-served sectors like SMEs as they provide efficient payment services to the public and maintain the safety of its savings. Ever-increasing speculative activity in the securities market serves no useful purpose and needs to be sharply curtailed. At the same time, rewards going to senior managers bear no relationship to social value addition and aggravate inequality. Such practices are bad examples for other sectors of the economy and should be contained. A major reform effort is needed for the financial sector across the world to make it more responsive to the needs of society and this effort will have to be driven by the State.

Keywords Political economy (P16) · Laissez faire (D62)
Private sector (P14) · Public interest (P43)

The preceding chapters have outlined the evolution and development of financial services, their role in economies at different levels of development and their contribution to an explosion of global indebtedness, both public and private, since the 1980s. An attempt has also been made to assess their role in the years leading up to the financial crisis of 2007/08. The discussion has also by way of background considered the complex relationship of money, saving and investment with the real economy and

S. Ahmed, *Ruling or Serving Society?*,
https://doi.org/10.1007/978-3-030-00521-4_5

has attempted to form a judgement, inter alia, about the pros and cons of an economy having a large financial sector and the risks generated by over-leveraging, matters articulated by Hyman Minsky and others more than 50 years ago. All this has been sought to be put in the context of the wider crisis of capitalism that has become visible since 2008. In this concluding chapter, we must now grapple with the question of where we go from here, say, over the next 15–20 years. In particular, we need to ask: what lessons have been learnt from the financial crisis, unprecedented in the severity of its long-term repercussions since the Great Depression of 1929, and what should be the role of a reformed financial sector in the wider scheme of things.

No one can doubt the pivotal role that finance plays in a modern economy and its contribution to economic and financial stability has been the subject of numerous inquiries stretching back almost a hundred years. But can, or should, things carry on broadly as they have over the last 10 years? Or, should finance be subjected to radical treatment not only to make it safer, which is the current preoccupation, but to seek to align it more directly with the longer-term interests and objectives of society that can be best summarized as sustainable, inclusive, equitable growth and development. The latter question arises within a larger set of issues: are economic systems to be taken as given, essentially unalterable, or are they there to satisfy the needs of society that include social justice and therefore subject to some form of democratic control (Norfield 2016).

Background and Overview

Following several reports after the 2007/08 crisis in the USA (2011), UK (2011) and at the BIS (2010), the current state of play is that a long drawn-out reform process is underway internationally at the BIS and in individual countries. The core objective of the effort is to make financial services safer for society in the post-crisis world by defining the risks emanating from moral hazard more strictly and reducing, if not eliminating, tax-funded bailouts for the sector in the future. Thus far, at any rate, there does not, however, appear to be much appetite for radical action. This is an understandable short-term reaction to the 2007/08 crisis on the part of governments who have attempted to portray it as serious but manageable. It conveys the generally complacent political mood in the developed countries. However, it is not going to be enough. Given the internal dynamics of finance and with indebtedness mounting once more, observers not only fear another crisis occurring sooner or later but also feel that most central banks and governments are ill-equipped to tackle it.[1] A further problem is that major financial institutions continue to exploit regulatory loopholes by incorporating subsidiaries and affiliates in lightly supervised locations and in tax havens. In other words, operations are still being kept opaque and regulatory arbitrage exploited as and when needed. International reform efforts have paid little or no attention to this aspect of finance so that in reality neither regulators nor the general public are any more aware of the internal mechanics of finance than they were in 2006.

So, the answer to the first question is that things cannot carry on as before. Over the long term, what is needed is not only to make finance safer but to find a way to reduce its deleterious impact such as the regular creation of asset bubbles leading to systemic instability, and to tackle the blatant ills financial services willy-nilly inflict on society, such as facilitating massive rent-seeking and the gross economic and social inequality that rent-seeking has generated in turn.[2] For these reasons, it is vital to make finance subservient to the needs of society. Safety is important but a radical programme of reform is also needed whereby finance is brought under greater social control that includes addressing the issues confronting capitalism that have been bubbling under the surface for some time but came to the fore after 2007/08.

One of the striking phenomena of the 1980s and 1990s is how finance came to dominate both developed and developing economies. How did economies allow finance to become so powerful? Part of the answer lies in the fact that over the last three decades finance itself has been at the forefront of promoting the mystique associated with self-regulating markets delivering optimal outcomes as part of the post-1980 neoliberal narrative. Epithets like 'masters of the universe' and

[1]The world has experienced a long period of ultra-low interest rates and QE. In the event of a new crisis central banks would have few, if any, means to tackle it.

[2]The World Inequality Report from the Paris School of Economics that came out in mid-December 2017 has made the point that current levels of inequality in the developed countries are not compatible with democracy. Social stability is only possible when the majority believe that the rich are pulling their weight in addressing the challenges confronting the world including that of inequality. The current stability is fragile and stashing assets in tax havens will be of little use in the event of a major socio-political breakdown in the global economy.

assertions that Goldman Sachs runs the world may be caricatures but they nevertheless also convey what for many are uncomfortable truths reflecting the extraordinary power wielded over society by finance. Governments, think tanks, the media and ordinary individuals are equally in its thrall fascinated by the vast rewards that financial companies seem to have conjured out of the thin air. For too many, both observers and participants in the day-to-day operations of the real economy, financial services appear to have become a world unto themselves entitled not just to special treatment by regulators and policy-makers but to a hands-off approach even on the part of society—a phenomenon starkly brought to light in the way that finance has been able to water down the reform efforts of the last few years.[3]

In creating this aura of exaggerated deference, finance has undoubtedly been given a strong helping hand by the media. A considerable proportion of the output of the media—TV, newspapers, professional journals and their various pundits—is saturated with information pertaining to the daily ups and downs of the financial markets often in barely decipherable language to the layperson. And a much-repeated incantation in the media is how all this is the result of the collective wisdom of markets. Thus, for example, the phenomenon known as 'bond market vigilantism' embodied in the ideal of 'sound public finance' has created a widespread and wholly irrational fear of budget deficits virtually across the whole world. All public spending is now viewed with the utmost suspicion with markets supposed to be all-knowing.

Sound public finance, a notion that is itself incapable of objective definition or measurement, effectively means no, or very small, budget deficits (the modus operandi of the WB, IMF and ADB for many years) combined with ever lower taxation, limited government and in the UK to virtually perpetual austerity based on the ludicrous notion of equating the government's finances with those of ordinary households. In other words, for bond market vigilantes, when it comes to public spending the judgements of markets are considered akin to forces of nature or even divine judgements and cannot, indeed, should not, be defied or ignored even when they encroach on matters to do with critical public policy choices. As a sop, neoliberalism offers that markets

[3] It is only in December 2017, 10 years after the crisis, that the capital adequacy provisions of Basel III have been approved but will not take effect until 2027. Many observers fear that the capital adequacy provisions will be almost certainly diluted in the meantime.

will eventually deliver the best outcomes in terms of resource allocation and overall societal prosperity. All that is needed is patience. Those who might quibble with these views are simply told to accept them as self-evident truths and take refuge in a kind of *Panglossian* optimism in which eventually all will be to the good. It is striking to note how both developed and developing countries have accepted the neoliberal narrative. It is not difficult to understand why. Neoliberalism sits very neatly with the interests of ruling elites everywhere as it seems to provide 'scientific' justification for low taxes on income and wealth.

But, in point of fact, all this goes against empirical knowledge. Whatever the proponents of neoliberal ideas might claim, financial services have delivered very little over the last three decades even before the 2007/08 events. In developed countries, finance in its search for profits has evolved into a form of gambling via securitization and the resultant massive expansion of trading in securities. In developing countries, by enabling gains obtained through the control and trading of scarce assets to be captured internally, finance has become the preferred vehicle for rent-seeking, sometimes blatantly in the shape of loan write-offs for friends and cronies. But, as we look ahead to the future and as the barely discernible, disruptive impacts of new technology become more apparent, the role of finance, too, will come under new pressure. It will need to take on the far bigger challenges of huge upheavals arising out of pressures in the jobs market, populism, paralysed politics and an ineffective state. How will the sector cope with these myriad sources of uncertainty in its *modus operandi* and be able to assess risk and creditworthiness realistically?

It is worth recalling again that traditionally the role of finance was to intermediate between savers and investors. The oversight and regulation of finance were in the hands of the central bank for the banking system and there was a separate agency for the securities markets. In the traditional oversight arrangements, central banks had much the more important role involving the safety and stability of the financial system and providing liquidity at critical moments to the economy. Their responsibilities ranged from preventing panics in the banking system, keeping inflation under control and promoting the fullest use of society's resources, particularly labour. However, the truth is that every 10 years or so economies had to confront major problems associated with instability in the financial sector leading to significant slowdowns in the economy and rising unemployment as regulators and governments dealt with the impact of asset bubbles, bad debts and illiquid or insolvent institutions. In 2007/08, central banks and others completely failed to foresee the gravity of the crisis building up with the reckless expansion of sub-prime mortgages and the issuance of CDOs. If the objective of reform is to provide a safer, i.e. more risk averse *and* a more socially responsible system for the future we must understand what is wrong with finance as currently organized.

Neoliberalism and Finance

In the early 1980s as the neoliberal world view became the prevailing economic narrative, the deregulation of finance was its central component. Deregulation meant that financial institutions were able to grow into behemoths and the rewards going to their senior managers reached astronomical levels. Finance acquired a special status not only in the eyes of the public but in think tanks as well and Economics itself was heavily influenced by this development taking the view that neoliberalism represented some kind of value-free science. In other words, the economy could be left to the operations of markets and if the government was going to intervene it would have to do so only within that conceptual framework. As finance grew in size with every passing year, it is hardly surprising that the sector began to believe that it *was* a world unto itself. It was argued that its greatly enhanced role was underpinned by the judgements of infallible markets and its inner workings required knowledge of advanced mathematics.

Other social sciences became no more than pale imitations of this allegedly rigorous combination of empiricism and logic. The sector was helped in this vain self-regard by over-indulgent regulators who, too, had bought into the need for deregulation with enthusiasm as part of the neoliberal construct. Deregulation also meant the downgrading of traditional finance and the rise to pre-eminence of wholesale banks dealing primarily with other banks and the issuance and trading of securities became the core activity. In this belief system, there was a further presumption that if there were instances of financial instability, or even failure of particular institutions, markets themselves, and not regulators, would deal with such events and their after-effects. Indeed, it was claimed that there were mathematical models to prove that this was the case.

One practical consequence of deregulation was that, operationally, financial institutions began to run with low levels of liquidity and high levels of leveraging. This meant that the failure of one institution could generate a domino-like effect on the rest of the sector, inevitably necessitating the intervention of the government to save the system from complete collapse. The question that arises is why were such obvious risks not better appreciated by regulators? With the benefit of hindsight, the answer lies in a simple explanation: regulators were equally seduced by developments in financial theory, that securitization, structuring of debt and derivatives would enable any given individual institution to fine-tune its desired combination of risk and return. Financial institutions could now both *increase* credit creation and *reduce* riskiness. None other than Alan Greenspan, Chairman of the Federal Reserve System of the USA noted in 2005 that derivatives were one of the key factors underlying the resilience of the banking system. A gullible public, an uncritical media and acquiescent research institutes were happy to go along with these comforting notions. If you add to that belief system elements of greed and hubris a dangerous cocktail of excessive and ill-understood risks in finance emerges that neither the senior managers of the major financial institutions nor their regulators had the ability to manage.

From Hyman Minsky and James Tobin to a host of other economists and financial experts (more recently Haldane 2010; Kay 2015; Turner 2016; Pettifor 2017; Foroohar 2016, to name only a few) have attempted to assess the true importance of financial services in an economy. The subject is complex and the information that the sector generates as to its profitability capable of widely differing interpretations. But, it is now generally accepted that value-added in finance, roughly the difference between the cost of its liabilities and the profits it earns on its assets and through its trading activities, as a measure of its contribution to the economy, is misleading. *First*, the sector hardly fits the textbook model of a competitive activity. Indeed, signs of cartel-like behaviour are readily apparent with significant levels of rent-seeking disguising value-added in the sector. Cartels and oligopolies exist in other sectors of the economy, too, but profits in sectors, such as manufacturing, are limited by the physical production of goods. In the trading of securities such constraints do not apply; the same security can be traded several times in a single day, each time adding to someone's trading profits and to a massive inflation of profits in the sector as a whole. *Second*, profitability can be routinely over-stated both by creative accounting and by excessive risk-taking—not forgetting, in this regard, the perverse incentives given to senior management in the sector for the exercise of stock options which encourages price manipulation. *Third*, while value-added in the sector may well approximate to profits within it, this value-added contributing little, if anything, to meeting wider societal needs. Indeed, a substantial chunk of the value-added is captured by senior managements within the sector. *Fourth*, the internalization of the added value is possible only because the notion 'too big to fail' allows senior managers to take excessive risks thus enabling them to capture the implicit subsidy that central banks and governments provide to the sector in the form of guarantees against insolvency. This is gambling effectively financed by society.

In an ideal world, unregulated finance run by talented managers and incentivized by the profit motive would maximize efficiency, as it does in other sectors of the economy, and lead to an optimal allocation of resources in the economy as a whole. But, we do not live in an ideal world. We live in a world where efficiency has been dangerously compromised by the penchant for herd-like behaviour in finance and where ultimate safety has been out-sourced to society so that even not-so-talented managers have been able to act with a casual disregard for the consequences of their actions. The traditional role of finance was to intermediate between the flow of funds amongst businesses and households. Now it constitutes only a tiny proportion of its balance sheet and daily activities. The overwhelming activity of finance of institutions is placing funds with other institutions that are then used for high volume trading in a variety of securities, including bizarre practices like spoofing, as discussed elsewhere in the book. Often the securities, e.g. stocks and bonds, are overlaid with other securities called derivatives, so described because their values are derived from these underlying securities. Trading in these securities carries no social utility beyond some alleged contribution to the price discovery process for the underlying stocks and bonds. But, on the contrary, it increases, and has been seen to increase, systemic risk exponentially. It is true that modern societies cannot function without access to finance. This does not mean that the more finance there is the better and certainly not the speculative finance that consists of trading in the securities markets including such dubious practices as short selling.[4]

[4]One product used in securities trading in the financial sector is the binary option. What it boils down to in simple terms is predicting whether the price of a share, commodity, currency or index is going to move up or down in the future. The future can be as little as 30 seconds and without sophisticated IT systems such trading would be impossible

Financialization: A Major Challenge

Earlier chapters have talked about the phenomenon of financialization that now bedevils a variety of economies. The term financialization has no convenient, off-the-peg operational definition. What it refers to is the marked increase in the size of the financial sector vis-à-vis other sectors of the economy. It also embodies the growing interdependence between many different institutions within economies and globally. Only 30–40 years ago a single financial enterprise in difficulties usually produced limited repercussions even within the sector and certainly not in the wider economy. This is no longer true. The insolvency of one institution can effectively cause the entire sector to freeze up.

While access to finance has widened significantly in society, the process of financialization itself, however, has been a source of gratuitous instability. Because of IT, financial activities are so closely enmeshed that problems multiply much faster than human managers can foresee. In fact, close examination of the financial system suggests that efforts to enhance the safety of one institution could actually make the system as a whole more risk-prone. For instance, during the 2007/08 crisis assets of questionable provenance were constantly shifted between institutions. This created an illusion of active management by institutions to prepare for the worst. In reality, it had the opposite effect of dispersing questionable assets across the system so that when one institution went into difficulties the whole system was affected. In fact, increasing financialization has produced substantial, negative side-effects for economies as a whole. Combined with globalization, financialization can potentially seize up large chunks of financial services in different parts of the world with devastating effects on the real economy.

In the UK, for example, private investment in plant, machinery, retraining and R&D has been weak because of the opportunities provided by speculation in the securities markets (Lapavitsas 2016; Onaran 2017). In fact, it would not be wrong to say that the rapid decline of manufacturing in the UK has been aided by the diversion of capital from upgrading manufacturing facilities and investing in new technology and

thus negating one of the critical props of the neoliberal belief system of perfect markets. There are moves now at the European Securities and Markets Authority and the Financial Conduct Authority in the UK to ban what is in effect gambling.

related sectors to speculation in the stock, bond and commodity markets. This has led to weak productivity growth not just in manufacturing but in the economy as a whole. As many observers have begun to notice, a redistribution of national income in favour of capital and away from labour has had the effect of initiating a vicious cycle of weak overall demand, lower domestic consumption and lower investment in the economy. The phenomenon of enterprises directing their profits to speculation in finance in the face of weak demand growth in the economy is *both a consequence* and *a cause* of the weak demand. In the past, the UK relied on rising wages to aid recovery after a recession. Following the last recession, recovery has been extraordinarily weak as instead of wages and productivity growth the country is witnessing another increase in household debt. A process of de-financialization thus has to be part of any reform effort and involves stronger regulation of the financial activities of non-financial enterprises.

What about the impact of new technology? Over the years, finance does not have an impressive record of dealing with the impact of new technology on the economy and society. In the IT-related boom at the turn of the Millennium, there were few, if any, voices in finance that attempted to dampen the public's enthusiasm for IT-related stock. The resultant stock market boom was followed by the inevitable bust and a recession that was, however, mercifully short-lived. The 2007/08 financial crisis was not driven by technology per se but had the same underlying belief of vast profits that would continue to be generated by enterprises and herd instinct and clever instruments like CDOs did the rest. Today's new technologies, for instance AI and robotics, are once again being seen as harbingers of a brave new world in which labour will be replaced by machines that will deliver progressively higher levels of profits and profitability in a variety of industries and services. Moreover, capital itself is going to be increasingly in a disembodied form and not in the form of physical plant and equipment. The real question that finance must grapple with is how to ensure that the new technologies do not intensify the 'winner-takes-all' phenomenon in society where wages continue to stagnate and owners of capital enrich themselves and contribute further to the forces of inequality. In such a scenario financial services will cease to have any meaningful role in society and will come to be seen as sophisticated parasites. Moreover, if their role is merely to intensify any passing fad and not to dampen the irrational exuberance that affects financial markets from time to time then the fight against instability is effectively lost.

Where Do We Go from Here?

There is palpable and justified unease across the world today that few governments appreciate the risks that a hugely leveraged economy poses for wider financial, economic and social stability. However, an acquiescent media is happy to downplay or even ignore the unease. In the UK, for instance, the City enjoys an extraordinary pre-eminence in the economy with an uncritical media its biggest cheerleader. Given this background, a fundamental question that must be asked today is about the need and justification of a massive financial sector for an average economy and society, in view of the risks that it poses to both on account of its size and activities. It has to be said, too, that allocating capital efficiently does not seem to be such a difficult job to justify the enormous financial rewards that senior managements of banks give themselves.

As of 2016, the vast size and complexity of financial services defy any rational explanation except as a vehicle for fuelling nth degree casino-like speculation in the securities and foreign exchange markets. This is especially visible in the context of the growing disconnect between the real economy and the financial sector. Economies are awash with liquidity yet vital productive activities are struggling for support. Moreover, the availability of liquidity not only encourages speculation and fuels volatility in the financial sector; it generates no countervailing benefits in the price discovery or capital allocation process in the financial markets—their supposed economic rationale—and market failures in the real economy are as widespread as ever. Above all, the savings of the public are no safer today, or being put to better use, than they were 25 years ago.

More fundamentally, questions need to be asked about the contribution of the financial sector in increasing wealth and income inequality in society and ultimately undermining democratic accountability. Indeed, no one can explain why tax havens continue to flourish in the world despite all the harm that they do to both developed and developing economies by allowing tax avoidance and by facilitating capital flight. Thus, side by side with the phenomenon of 'secular stagnation' the world is having to confront a daunting array of political and social problems for which most governments have little or no appetite to take the necessary action if it involves taking on strongly entrenched corporate and political interests.

What then of the next 10–15 years? *First*, steps should be taken to engineer a tamer and smaller financial sector starting with the separation of retail from investment banking. A smaller financial sector in order to reduce the vulnerability that high levels of leveraging create for the rest of the economy does appear to be happening now but much too slowly. It is also worth noting that retail banking plays the role of a utility in a modern economy and as such it could—and perhaps should—function in the public domain. Neoliberals would find such a notion almost impossible to countenance but many countries manage to function quite well with an essentially publicly owned retail banking sector. Alternatively, a larger number of smaller banks might reduce systemic risk and enhance competitive pressure in finance, another no-go area for neoliberals who tend to think that markets always deliver the best outcomes and large banks are better than small ones.

Second, within the retail sector, a BCCI-like institution, with extensive coverage in the developing countries, is clearly needed to replicate the functions of, say, the German *landsbanken*. Access to short term or trade finance is not the main gap in financial services in the developing countries but longer-term support is. What broad-based development needs is access to stable long-term finance without the gratuitous volatility that speculation inevitably creates in financial markets and then irrationally magnifies from time to time. Neither economic growth nor development has any need for speculative activities, however technically sophisticated in terms of their mathematics.

Third, other needs are more efficient international payments systems between developing countries, more non-traditional finance for trade between the developed and developing countries and for far larger volumes of infrastructure and project financing than are currently available. Backed by the huge foreign exchange reserves of the developing countries a new institution perhaps operating with a synthetic unit of account could provide a new impetus to trade and other forms of liquidity support for greater interaction between developing countries. The Chinese-led Asian Infrastructure Investment Bank is a step in the right direction. It ought to be replicated by similar institutions at the country level.

These are complex and important elements in what is patently a long overdue reform process for banking and for the wider financial services sector and they apply equally to developed and developing economies. In the UK, for example, mortgage finance not only dominates banking but has made banks overly risk-averse in offering other types of lending. Small- and medium-sized businesses requiring longer-term support have few avenues that they can use. It is therefore unlikely that leaving such reforms to the calculus of the private sector and to the untrammelled operations of markets would meet these needs. Indeed, experience with the financialization of economies since the 1990s has made the problem a good deal worse but the 2007/08 debacle in the banking systems of many countries indicates that change is both needed and is possible.

It will need to be reiterated that by engaging in speculation, financial markets not only pre-empt resources at a massive scale but also create risks in case of losses that neither shareholders nor regulators have the capacity to bear. There is a general presumption that ultimately any losses in the future will again have to be made good, as in the wake of the 2007/08 crisis, by the taxpayers. Such a solution is neither practical nor morally justifiable. What the financial sector actually does is to aggravate/intensify existing trends through herd instinct in the securities markets. It thus adds to, and does not reduce, instability. Society should not have to bale it out again and again.

In attempting to answer the questions that have arisen in the preceding discussion, three sets of basic objectives should be at the forefront. *First,* finance has to be cut down to size and an immediate step in that direction is to separate retail from wholesale banking, as was initially proposed in Basel III and was the case prior to 1987. An over-large financial sector has led to over-leveraging at a massive scale with all its attendant dangers. A smaller financial sector will create a better balance between debt and equity in the economy by reducing unnecessary leveraging and mitigate the impact of failure. Likewise, bloated individual institutions that have created the self-serving idea of 'too big to fail' need to be broken up into their separate functional spheres and, perhaps, also geographically.

Reform should aim to minimize, if not remove, the implicit subsidy available to banks in the form of State guarantees against insolvency and retail banking that primarily provides payment services to households and firms could easily be in the public domain as used to be the case with all utilities. In addition to the separation of retail from wholesale banking and a severe curtailment of securities trading through much higher capital buffers, the *second* objective should be anchoring finance explicitly to the needs of society. This objective, while self-evident, requires explanation. Believers in markets will argue that the arrangements already ensure this as markets provide saving and investment outlets with the full range of liquidity and time preferences, the so-called Arrow–Debreu 'states of nature' (1954). However, despite the rise of securities' trading on a vast scale, this is patently not the case. The securities markets merely provide betting odds with respect to the *events* that will, in turn, affect prices.in these markets; they do not give any clues as to the determination of the actual prices of the underlying securities in the first place based on their earnings potential over the long term.

It is worth reiterating here that at the level of households, the everyday needs of society consist of an efficient payments mechanism so that payments for the ordinary day-to-day activities of consumers can be performed safely. Society also needs access to temporary loans to smooth the natural time variations between earnings and expenditures that occur and for emergencies—say, the equivalent of an overdraft facility. This is currently provided by expensive credit cards and even higher cost payday loans that lock people into permanent debt and is the cause of much family and social distress. Households also need sound professional advice and help at reasonable cost to save, especially at a time when the old social contract with respect to corporate pensions based on final earnings has all but broken down and State provision of pensions is hopelessly inadequate. At the level of the providing help to firms or enterprises, the financial sector has to develop a much more long-term perspective.

As said earlier, the conventional role of finance was the provision of working capital to enterprises for the purchase of raw material before production or the financing of inventory before sale, once the initial investment had been made. Nowadays, the reality is that enterprises get little or no help from the financial sector in this area and are often left looking for new equity partners. Furthermore, it is not simply a question of providing finance. Sound advice and sensitive market intelligence in a wide range of economic sectors are likely to be equally useful and the finance sector has either allowed such skills to deteriorate over the years or only provides them at high cost. It is known that SMEs are the engines of most economies but their needs have been conspicuously neglected by finance.

Another enterprise sector that requires help is start-ups. Start-ups are the backbone of any economy but the finance sector has developed no institutional support for start-ups, leaving them to the mercy of private equity funds. The latter either have a narrow, very short-term view of the potential of start-ups or demand excessive concessions from their promoters. In some developing countries, the government provides limited assistance in the form of guarantees to SMEs and start-ups. There is clearly a case for such assistance to be scaled up and for this policy and regulatory intervention will be needed.

By and large, financial services prefer to cater to already established large enterprises or to the needs of wealthy households. While this is justifiable on the grounds of creditworthiness it has not prevented individual institutions from making spectacular blunders. Indeed, concentrating risk in a few large accounts is a recipe for disaster and securitization has hardly helped matters. The penalties incurred by banks in the aftermath of the financial crisis are an object lesson for those who think that wealth, securitisation and low risk are coterminous. Nevertheless, finance has gone into securities trading to an extraordinary degree and a high proportion of financial sector revenues and profits originate in securities' trading. The profitability of these activities has been built upon complex tax and legal arrangements, barriers to entry and cartel-like collusion that almost inexorably leads to the rigging of markets. These roles have attracted not only huge capital, financial and human, but also massive investments in IT systems. The real question that needs answering is whose needs are being satisfied in this way? The answer must be no one other than the institutions themselves and, perhaps, some of their wealthy clients. The primary purpose of finance here appears to be to benefit the various intermediaries that operate these services and certainly not their end-users. And in this context, it should not be forgotten that all the money that circulates in the financial system is money that belongs to the general public. Traditionally, the safety of the money was taken with the utmost seriousness. Nowadays, as 'too big to fail' has become the operative reality, moral hazard has taken over and reckless risk-taking has become the norm. Functionally, i.e. seen from the perspective of society, speculative trading need not exist at all as it performs no socially useful function.

The *third* objective of reform is to identify the practical value-adding role that finance plays in the economy and to strengthen it. For much of the nineteenth century and almost to the end of the 1970s, finance did play the role assigned to it as summarized in Economics textbooks. This consisted of a payments system for households and enterprises domestically and across borders to carry out their day-to-day activities and the provision of finance for trade and of loans, usually short term, to individuals and businesses. For those who needed long-term support wholesale finance, like merchant and investment banks, provided access to the stock and bond markets. A subsidiary function that also grew over time was the organization and management of saving and pension schemes and carrying out fund and investment management on behalf of wealthy clients. However, all these roles have been put in the shade by the magnitude of dealings *between* financial institutions that are mostly used for the creation of ever more esoteric securities and trading in these securities.

The financial sector will have to learn to recognize the long-term importance of the physical production of goods in the economy—this was the traditional function of finance until the 1980s. Finance must surely return to its traditional roots so that it can play its proper role in the economy supporting production and smaller, less creditworthy enterprises and by taking a more forward-looking strategic view of the constantly changing economic environment. Building an enterprise for the long term requires long-term support. Banks need to be better equipped to deliver such support.

The reform process embodied in the Basel Committee on Banking Supervision—otherwise known as Basel III—has thus far concentrated attention on strengthening microprudential regulation and supervision and has recommended raising equity capital and liquidity to a much higher level than was the case before 2007. It has also made recommendations regarding leverage and risk. However, it leaves the weeding out of risk-taking institutions from the rest to the market and it does not consider how under-served areas of the economy can have better access to finance. In other words, it takes an essentially hands-off approach to reform with little in the way of guidance with regard to the kind of questions that have been raised in the preceding paragraphs. From a forward-looking perspective what the reform process should now seek to achieve, as stated elsewhere, is a smaller finance sector with smaller institutions within it.

A parallel objective of reform should lie in what used to be called 'moral suasion'. In the past, the power of moral suasion allowed central banks to issue private guidance to individual institutions taking too many risks. In today's world regulators should raise the fiduciary obligations of financial institutions to a more explicit, formalized pre-eminence, a simple enough requirement but one which is currently observed in the breach. Fiduciary duties have been effectively obscured to vanishing point by the extraordinary complexity of the overall system. The complexity is a deliberately created phenomenon, unnecessary in its overall rationale, but useful for camouflaging what is going on in any institution at any given time. Neither senior managers within the institution nor its external inspectors and regulators can be expected to have a clear view of the activities that are taking place under their notional purview. For the former, if short-term profits are being made that is good enough; for the latter, bland assurances from the institutions that all is well are usually sufficient, stress tests or no.

The complexity of the modern economy and of its various sectors has largely gone hand in hand with economic growth since World War II and the rapid development of IT systems. But there comes a point when the expense of managing such a system and the information that it generates becomes too much and leads to dysfunction. Furthermore, complex IT systems are not only difficult to manage but are prone to breakdown and to seizing up, however robust their design. In the wake of the 2007/08 crisis, a body for the separate oversight of banks has been set up in many countries, for instance the UK, with central banks entrusted with the formulation and management of monetary policy. This separation of responsibilities has not yet been tested by a major crisis; therefore, it would be premature to comment upon its appropriateness or effectiveness as a reform measure.

Before any reform effort can be initiated its case will have to be won at the intellectual level that financial markets are not repositories of wisdom and restrictions need to be placed on them in the longer-term interests of society. Unchecked speculation, far from serving any useful purpose, is a recipe for disaster both at the technical level in that it nearly always ends in failure and at the moral level as it encourages unsavoury human traits such as grasping behaviour whose side effects can be devastating for the rest of society. How this can be done is unlikely to be straightforward as any attempts at modifying human nature towards greater social responsibility are almost certain to provoke opposition if not ridicule. Those who regard markets as sacrosanct are unlikely to be impressed.

Conclusions

In considering the ultimate objectives of the reform process for financial services, it would be well to bear in mind that the market and private sector-driven model that most countries have been functioning with has itself lost much of its legitimacy post 2007/08. Fundamentally, extant economic systems have fallen well short in the fairness of their rewards for the different factors of production in an economy. Levels of inequality and, by the same token, the absence of any countervailing arrangements for the provision of social protection and public goods have reached levels that were last seen almost a hundred years ago. It appears as if the egalitarian instincts that contributed to the strength, stability and dynamism of the post-1945 sociopolitical consensus have become fatally eroded. The erosion of these instincts raises issues relating to political economy and the role of fiscal policy, especially in the areas of personal and corporate taxation and in the overall management of the economy. In this, it should be stressed, issues of political economy are never too far from the prevailing moral climate (Plender 2015; Standing 2016; Varoufakis 2017). Even Adam Smith who first enunciated the efficacy of the invisible hand of the market in satisfying the needs of society was aware that society also needed the rudder of 'moral sentiments' to guide it through the choppy seas of unrestrained profit-maximizing behaviour. Currently, the rudder appears to be malfunctioning and is leading society into ever more dangerous waters.

The wider philosophical issue facing all of us is to examine the value system whereby we attempt to understand and justify the processes that enable society to function and for the economy to satisfy the needs of society. All the different elements that allow an economy to perform its tasks are there because they ultimately contribute to the welfare of society. Whatever their claims to the contrary, neither finance nor technology has any role independent of that test of legitimacy. It is well to remember, too, that while markets have proved to be useful vehicles for deploying the resources of society they are not proxies for its value system or for its long-term objectives and priorities.

The last decade or so has brought uncomfortably to light the unsavoury side of human nature embodied in the greed that characterized the doings of bankers, not just in precipitating the 2007/08 crisis but in almost system-wide malfeasance during and after the crisis. Large numbers seemed to be quite happy to play with other people's money in the pursuit of private gain. Other unsavoury traits that have been revealed are the lengths to which both corporations and wealthy individuals will go to avoid paying tax. The idea that unchecked greed and tax avoidance can be socially harmless defies elementary common sense. Tax avoidance, as opposed to tax evasion, is an activity in which financial services have been deeply complicit. What is forgotten in such behaviour is that large-scale tax avoidance not only puts in doubt the durability of the underlying social contract that determines how groups, vis-à-vis other groups, and individuals, vis-à-vis other individuals, conduct themselves but creates the problem of free-ridership. Widespread tax avoidance causes societies to lose a sense of cohesiveness, they then start to become atomized and are only a short distance away from disintegration.

We live today in a world beset by extraordinary uncertainty about the future, not least because of the manifest failures of neoliberal capitalism in failing to deliver equity in society. This version of capitalism with its internal dynamics of instability is contributing to a palpable sense of insecurity amongst both the young and the elderly, the former unable to find decently paid, fulfilling employment, the latter fearful of ending their lives in poverty. Even those with jobs enjoy a precarious existence, especially those who have been classified as self-employed primarily to give a false allure to the employment statistics. Finance's inability to rein in the forces of instability, combined with geopolitical uncertainty and democracy having been converted into unabashed plutocracy, has left few people with any confidence that much or, indeed, any improvement can be expected in the future.

In most countries, it is the State that will have to drive the reform effort. For the time being the needed political will based on a rational and frank realization of long-term societal needs is lacking. Instead, driven by the media and even by the so-called independent research institutes, ruling elites across the world cling tenaciously to an obsolete set of ideas based on neoliberal precepts. This does not suggest that politically powerful, narrow private interests will voluntarily satisfy the needs of society and create a smaller financial sector or, indeed, a more harmonious and fairer society in the process. Clearly, a great deal of work is needed to create and sustain the needed political will to this end. A major effort is therefore needed now at the G20 to devise a programme of reform for the financial sector. Stopping money laundering and terrorism financing is important but so is having a global financial sector that there is to serve society. The Financial Action Task Force (FATF) at the G7 could be replicated at the G20 for this purpose with effective developing country representation.

Above all, it must be asked: what is the financial sector ultimately for? Is it there to provide for the needs of society or is it there to manage the world's savings under private authority, largely unanswerable to any State institutions, for the benefit of a tiny elite? The 2007/08 crisis has exposed not just greed but a glaring lack of technical expertise in the sector and its claims that risk had been mastered have been exposed as hollow. In fact, senior managers in the sector, far from accepting responsibility, have been at pains to shift responsibility to others including the borrowers themselves but with weak regulation being their particular favourite.[5]

It is true that finance has not created the crisis of capitalism on its own. But it has contributed in significant ways to the current situation. And it is obvious that finance cannot be expected to remedy the ills of capitalism on its own. What it can do, however, is to stamp down on its own internal greed in the form of the vast salaries and bonuses that senior managers pay themselves and the blatant rent-seeking that it facilitates not only in its own sector but in the rest of the economy.[6] It might start by refusing to take part in the questionable transfers of money known as money-laundering by individuals and corporations. It might also cease giving help to those who make every effort to avoid paying taxes by creating bogus entities, such as trusts, in tax havens and mechanisms such as transfer prices for them. It can also give up its own use of tax havens.[7] With these measures, it would be better able to realize and accept its responsibilities as the honest guardian of society's savings and interests and not as one whose primary purpose is to exploit society and merely enrich the people who work in it.

[5]This is rather like criminals blaming laxity on the part of the police for their criminal behaviour.

[6]The vast rewards available to senior managers in financial services are in part driven by a strange reluctance on the part of society to call them what they actually are—a fairly brazen form of rent-seeking. In the UK, another remarkable manifestation of rent-seeking, such as the salaries of Vice Chancellors of Universities (twice those of equivalent officials in Germany), has few, if any, defenders and the intellectual argument in their favour has been lost.

[7]This notion will appear far-fetched to many. However, it is worth pointing out that the World Bank group has announced that it will end its support for oil and gas exploration within the next two years as part of the battle against climate change. The group has already ceased funding for coal-fired power stations. Pension funds are under similar pressure to play a more active role in countering climate change by reducing/eliminating their investments in CO_2-emitting industries. Would it be too much to ask that finance, too, takes steps along the lines outlined in this chapter towards playing a more socially responsible role in the global economy?

References

Arrow, K., & Debreu, G. (1954). Existence of an Equilibrium for a Competitive Economy. *Econometrica, 22*, 265–290.

Bank for International Settlements. (2010). *The Long-Term Impact of Stronger Capital and Liquidity Requirements*. Basel: BIS Committee on Banking Supervision.

Foroohar, R. (2016). *Makers and Takers: How Wall Street Destroyed Main Street*. New York: Crown Publishing Group.

Haldane, A. (2010). The Contribution of the Financial Sector: Miracle or Mirage. In Part of a co-authored chapter *The Future of Finance*, LSE Report, London.

Kay, J. (2015). *Other People's Money: Masters of the Universe or Servants of the People*. London: Profile Books.

Lapavitsas, C., & Mendieta-Munoz, I. (2016). The Profits of Financialisation. *Monthly Review* (pp. 49–62). New York, NY.

Norfield, T. (2016). *The City: London and the Global Power of Finance*. London: Verso.

Onaran, O., & Tori, D. (2017). *Productivity Puzzle? Financialisation, Inequality and Investment in the UK*. Policy Brief 16-2017, University of Greenwich Political Economy Research Centre, London.

Pettifor, A. (2017). *The Production of Money: How to Break the Power of Bankers*. London: Verso.

Plender, J. (2015). *Capitalism, Money, Morals and Markets*. London: Biteback Publishing.

Standing, G. (2016). *The Corruption of Capitalism: Why Rentiers Thrive and Work Does Not Pay*. London: Biteback Publishing.

Turner, A. (2016). *Between Debt and the Devil: Money, Credit, and Fixing Global Finance*. Princeton: Princeton University Press.

Varoufakis, Y. (2017). *And the Weak Suffer What They Must*. London: Vintage.

Bibliography

Arrow, K., & Debreu, G. (1954). Existence of an Equilibrium for a Competitive Economy. *Econometrica, 22,* 265–290.

Bank for International Settlements. (2010). *The Long-Term Impact of Stronger Capital and Liquidity Requirements.* Basel: BIS Committee on Banking Supervision.

Foroohar, R. (2016). *Makers and Takers: How Wall Street Destroyed Main Street.* New York: Crown Publishing Group.

Genberg, H. (2015, December). Capital Market Development and Emergence of Institutional Investors in the Asia-Pacific Region. *UN ESCAP Asia-Pacific Development Journal, 22,* 1–32.

Haldane, A. (2010). The Contribution of the Financial Sector: Miracle or Mirage. In Part of a co-authored chapter *The Future of Finance*, LSE Report, London.

Independent Commission on Banking. (2011). *Interim Report: Consultation on Reform Options.* London: Victoria House.

Kay, J. (2015). *Other People's Money: Masters of the Universe or Servants of the People.* London: Profile Books.

Khwaja, A., & Mian, A. (2011). Rent-Seeking and Corruption in Financial Markets. *Annual Review of Economics, 3,* 579–600.

Lapavitsas, C., & Mendieta-Munoz, I. (2016). The Profits of Financialisation. *Monthly Review* (pp. 49–62). New York, NY.

Lazonick, W. (2010). Innovative Business Models and Varieties of Capitalism: Financialization of the US Corporation. *Business History Review, 84*(4), 675–702.

Lazonick, W. (2014, September). Profits Without Prosperity. *Harvard Business Review.*

S. Ahmed, *Ruling or Serving Society?*,
https://doi.org/10.1007/978-3-030-00521-4

Llanto, G., Navarro, A., & Ortiz, M. K. (2015, December). Infrastructure Financing, Public-Private Partnerships and Development in the Asia-Pacific Region. *UN ESCAP Asia-Pacific Development Journal*, *22*(2), 27–70.

Mian, A., & Sufi, A. (2014). *House of Debt: How They Caused the Great Recession and How We Can Prevent It from Happening Again.* Chicago: University of Chicago Press.

Miller, S. M., & Upadhyay, M. P. (2000, December). The Effects of Openness, Trade Orientation and Human Capital on Total Factor Productivity. *Journal of Development Economics, 63,* 399–423.

Minsky, H. (1992). *The Financial Stability Hypothesis* (Working Paper 74). Annadale-on-Hudson, NY: Levy Economics Institute.

Norfield, T. (2016). *The City: London and the Global Power of Finance.* London: Verso.

Onaran, O., & Tori, D. (2017). *Productivity Puzzle? Financialisation, Inequality and Investment in the UK.* Policy Brief 16-2017, University of Greenwich Political Economy Research Centre, London.

Ostry, J., Loungani, P., & Furceri, D. (2016, June). *"Neoliberalism: Oversold?" Finance and Development.* Washington, DC: IMF.

Oxfam. (2017). *An Economy for the 99 Per Cent.* London: Oxfam.

Pettifor, A. (2017). *The Production of Money: How to Break the Power of Bankers.* London: Verso.

Plender, J. (2015). *Capitalism, Money, Morals and Markets.* London: Biteback Publishing.

Robinson, J. (1966). *An Essay on Marxian Economics* (2nd ed.). London: Macmillan (1st edition published in 1942).

Roll, E. (1962). *A History of Economic Thought.* London: Faber and Faber.

Silver, N. (2017). *Finance, Society and Sustainability: How to Make the Financial System Work for the Economy, People and Planet.* London: Palgrave Macmillan.

Standing, G. (2016). *The Corruption of Capitalism: Why Rentiers Thrive and Work Does Not Pay.* London: Biteback Publishing.

Storm, S. (2018). *Financial Markets Have Taken Over the Economy, to Prevent Another Crisis They Must Be Brought to Heel.* Institute for New Economic Thinking.www.inteconomics.org/perspectives/blog/financial-markets-have-taken-over-the.

The Economist. (2017, May 6–12). Special Report: International Banking.

Tobin, J. (1984). *On the Efficiency of the Financial System.* London: Lloyds Bank Review.

Turner, A. (2016). *Between Debt and the Devil: Money, Credit, and Fixing Global Finance.* Princeton: Princeton University Press.

US Federal Deposit Insurance Corporation. (2002). *The S and L Crisis: A Chrono-Bibliography.* Washington, DC: US Federal Deposit Insurance Corporation.

US Financial Crisis Inquiry Commission. (2011). *The Financial Crisis Inquiry Report*. Washington, DC: US Financial Crisis Inquiry Commission.

Varoufakis, Y. (2017). *And the Weak Suffer What They Must*. London: Vintage.

Vos, R., & Kozul-Wright, R. (2010). *Economic Insecurity and Development*. New York: United Nations.

Wolf, M. (2014). *Radical Reform for the Global Financial System*. US Council on Foreign Relations, C. Peter McColough Series on International Economics by the Corporate Program and Maurice Greenberg Center for Geoeconomic Sudies.

Index

A

Asset bubble, 15, 33, 40, 85, 88

B

Bank failures, 27, 34, 88, 95
Banking
 commercial, 3, 7, 38, 45
 investment, 6–11, 18, 21–26, 29, 32–35, 38, 40, 41, 43–46, 49, 52–57, 61, 68, 69, 71–73, 76, 77, 83, 91, 92, 94–98, 102
 retail, 6, 26, 32–35, 54, 71, 94, 95
 wholesale, 6, 10, 26, 32–34, 54, 71, 88, 95, 97
Banking principle, 2
Budget deficit, 23, 57, 86

C

Cartelization, 12, 62, 63
Central bank, 2, 3, 13, 16, 39–41, 57, 61, 85, 87, 88, 90, 98, 99
Choice, 16, 77, 78, 86
Credit rating, 7, 32

D

Derivatives, 8, 32, 35, 64, 89, 90

F

Factor rewards, 69
Fairness, 20, 26, 99
Financial crises, 39
Financialization, 5–7, 9, 25, 29, 31, 59, 63, 91, 92, 95
Financial markets, 7, 9, 12, 31, 32, 72, 86, 92–95, 99
Financial system, 3–5, 7, 8, 10, 11, 24, 33, 39, 44, 51, 74, 87, 91, 97
Forward and futures markets, 8

G

Globalization, 29, 33, 38, 41, 62, 91
Growth and development, 19, 41, 44, 46, 47, 49, 51, 53, 64, 84

H

Hedging, 8, 36, 45

S. Ahmed, *Ruling or Serving Society?*,
https://doi.org/10.1007/978-3-030-00521-4

I

Immigration, 9
Import-substituting strategy, 10
Infrastructure, 5, 10, 27, 28, 44, 45, 47, 51, 52, 55, 76, 77, 94
Instability, 6, 8, 9, 22, 28, 31, 40, 41, 72, 85, 87, 88, 91, 92, 95, 101
Intermediation, 12, 31, 33, 34, 44, 45, 49, 51, 55, 60, 64, 67
International integration, 11, 56
Intervention, 28, 30, 69, 71, 89, 97
Investment-GDP ratio, 11, 52, 72

K

Keynesian economics, 8

L

Laissez faire, 27–29
Leveraging, 89, 94, 95

M

Market failure, 13, 36, 73, 93
Mixed economies, 77
Monetary theory, 2, 16, 17
Money, 2–4, 8, 11–13, 15–18, 21, 23, 28, 31, 37, 39, 59, 62, 83, 97, 100, 102

O

Optimal outcomes, 78, 85

P

Paper money, 2, 17
Political economy, 20, 25, 26, 70, 100
Political ideology, 23, 25, 29, 70, 101
Price discovery, 19, 90, 93
Prices and relative prices, 5, 8, 16, 22, 23, 28, 34, 36, 38, 40, 51, 68, 69, 72, 96, 102
Price stability, 3, 21, 22, 27, 39, 41
Productivity, 18, 22, 45, 46, 48, 62, 69, 70, 92

R

Regulation, 2, 11, 16, 27–29, 33, 34, 37, 39, 57, 58, 60, 63, 69, 73, 87, 92, 98, 102
Rent, 5, 12, 32, 46, 48, 58, 60, 63, 64, 77, 80, 85, 87, 89, 102
Risk, 4–6, 8, 12, 18, 32, 33, 36, 44–46, 48, 57, 58, 60, 61, 63–65, 72, 87–91, 94, 97, 98, 101

S

Securities, 6, 7, 9, 10, 18, 19, 23, 25, 31, 34–36, 38, 39, 41, 48, 60–62, 87–91, 93, 95–98
Shares and bonds, 4, 5, 7, 19, 44
Social tensions, 9
State-owned enterprises, 51
States of nature, 11, 12, 95
Stock markets, 10, 18, 29, 31, 38, 51, 52, 54, 56
Surplus value, 20, 21

The manufacturer's authorised representative in the EU is Springer Nature Customer Service Centre GmbH, Europaplatz 3, 69115 Heidelberg, Germany. If you have any concerns regarding our products, please contact ProductSafety@springernature.com

Printed and bound by CPI Group (UK) Ltd, Croydon, CR0 4YY
30/09/2026
02225514-0002